Gita
Vedic & Wisdom

Greatest Spiritual Wisdom

PRANAY

BEL!EF

Reprint 2022

FiNGERPRINT! BELiEF

An imprint of Prakash Books India Pvt. Ltd.

113/A, Darya Ganj, New Delhi-110 002,
Tel: (011) 2324 7062 – 65, Fax: (011) 2324 6975
Email: info@prakashbooks.com/sales@prakashbooks.com

facebook www.facebook.com/fingerprintpublishing
twitter www.twitter.com/FingerprintP
www.fingerprintpublishing.com

ISBN: 978 93 5440 292 0

Processed & printed in India

The wise person lets go of all results,
whether good or bad,
and is focused on the action alone.

The Bhagavad Gita

Just as a bird uses two wings to fly, so too must we use
both the wing of spiritual knowledge and the wing of
dynamic action, to fulfil our lives!

Agastya Rishi, the great Vedic sage of ancient India

Preface

The Bhagavad Gita and Vedic teachings (the heart of Hinduism or Sanatan Dharma) are profound. They contain deep secrets for fearless and successful living, especially for dealing with tough times and crisis situations. This book is a distillation of the deepest lessons for true success in both the material and spiritual spheres of life, and for coping with circumstances of all sorts.

Containing mind-body-spirit teachings from India's rich spiritual heritage of thousands of years, the book is meant to be a practical guide as well as a mystical one. In an age of renewed global interest in yogic and Hindu philosophy, this book would be a timely resource for readers worldwide who seek to find a more spiritual approach to fearless success. It is imperative that the consciousness teachings and wisdom teachings of the Gita and Hinduism reach millions more, and become a force of greater good in the area of higher human success.

The language in the book has been purposely kept simple: very heavy classical Sanskrit has not been used, so that the book's core teachings are accessible to all.

Pranay

Contents

CHAPTER-1

Inspiration:
The Vishnu Key

Krishna—the speaker of the great scripture the Bhagavad Gita—is considered an avatar of Lord Vishnu or 'Narayan'. Narayan's primary function within the universe is to be the all-pervasive element of all things, the divine sustainer. And as the divine sustainer, Narayan is supposed to inspire all beings, is supposed to fill all beings with *prerna* or divine inspiration. This prerna or divine inspiration urges us to evolve. It stirs up the deepest psycho-spiritual impulses within mankind. And that is the whole function of the Bhagavad Gita. The Gita is meant to help the evolution of the individual called Arjun, but is also meant to inspire and deeply evolve humankind as a whole. When you understand it properly, the Gita creates the idea of spontaneous, spiritually inspired living within all of us. Spiritually inspired living is the key to fearless and successful living. It is the cornerstone of Hinduism or Sanatan Dharma (the ancient spiritual path). It creates dynamism within all life situations, tough times, and challenges.

Two Aspects of Krishna

To understand the Gita, we must understand two key things about the personality behind it: Krishna. The first thing is Krishna as 'Yogeshwara': the ultimate and most profound master/lord/teacher of inspiring yogic wisdom. The second thing is Krishna as 'Madhava': the one full of spiritual sweetness/ delight/charm, whose nectar-like message is to be heeded and enjoyed deep within ourselves, inspiring and awakening us to the highest happiness, bliss and ecstasy of living (as it is said: '*madhuradhipate akhilam madhuram*—everything about Krishna is divine sweetness). To understand both these inspirational aspects—of wisdom and delight—is to begin understanding the heart of Hindu spirituality. It explains the timeless inspiration of Vedic mysticism over the millennia, even to great scientific minds such as the quantum physicist Werner Heisenberg (who was profoundly moved and inspired after speaking to Rabindranath Tagore about deeper aspects of Hindu philosophy, and began to see the interconnectedness of all things). Hindu wisdom and Vedic knowledge hinge on divine inspiration at all levels: mystic, scientific, aesthetic, cosmic, and universal.

Arjun Symbolizes Us

Within the context of the Bhagavad Gita, we see that upon the battlefield of Kurukshetra stands the great warrior Arjun, seeking the inspiration and counsel of Krishna. Arjun represents the individual being beset with doubt, hopelessness, and anxiety. He is unable to fight, unable to decide what to do, unable to be his highest self. He is lost amidst a tough situation, confused and bewildered. His situation is looking difficult. His is a classical *'dharma-sankat'* or spiritual crisis, which we all face during moments of fear, uncertainty, and indecisiveness. Arjun is in the most uninspired state, and to lift him up to the highest spiritual inspiration is the point of Krishna's Gita!

Remember: all of us are 'Arjun', each one. Arjun is simply a metaphor for the individual soul who is interacting with the cosmic super-soul called Krishna or the great Vishnu avatar. Arjun symbolizes us. And Krishna's attitude is to help us move towards having an attitude of *nishkama bhava*: undertaking inspired action without expectation of results, while being inwardly relaxed in whatever one does, and being spontaneous. That reflects our true divine nature.

In a way, this idea has been the quest not just of Hinduism, but of all religions that have sprung out of India. The idea of spontaneous and inspired living: the idea of making your consciousness such that you are able to ignite your inner essence, your inner soul, of knowing its true oneness with the divine element. That is the whole secret of the Gita. That is also the quest of another avatar of Vishnu: Buddha. It is also the quest of the Tirthankaras of Jainism, of the gurus of Sikhism (starting with Guru

Nanak), of the Naths (starting with Matsyendranath, Gorakhnath, and others), and of literally all other paths of Indic origin.

There are several steps to spiritually inspired living, the first being the idea of the Gita that our psychological and physiological beings, while constituting our worldly 'self', never speak about our greater spiritual 'self' or soulful aspect. We have imprisoned ourselves with the thought that we are creatures of mind and body. We have to instead move towards realizing that tranquillity, that calmness of being which happens only when you realize that you are part and parcel of a greater existence. That way, two things happen: you start looking at yourself spiritually, and your fear of failure goes. And through that, you heal yourself at the level of mind-body-spirit and you start becoming inwardly powerful.

Inward Relaxation

Inward relaxation leads to inspired inward power. That is the whole meaning of the Bhagavad Gita. Ordinarily, we think the opposite, because in our world, we see people trying to attain meaning through outward, hectic activity. But really, you have to begin with a deep peace within your own being. Then all the other dimensions of life—your work within the world, your relationships, and so on—start improving. It is all about your spiritual energy within, which leads to that inspired living which Krishna is talking about.

Arjun's mind is such that it is running in different directions. It has not attained the calmness of being. Arjun has become paranoid. He's thinking about consequences. He's not able to rest in that nishkama bhava, that spontaneous, selfless idea of being and acting. That is what Krishna takes him towards. And when within himself Arjun settles—when his mind settles into the state of spontaneous and intimate understanding of the spiritual aspect of life—is when he starts acting dynamically also. That is when his highest virtues start surfacing.

The Purity of the Gita

The Gita does not go by any dogmas. It doesn't go by any belief. It is very pure! Krishna's work is to satisfy Arjun's questions not through belief systems, but through making him feel the essence of his own being, through making him see and perceive the truth on his own. And when we perceive the truth on our own, then we realize the courage within ourselves!

Krishna is a catalyst. Eventually, it is Arjun's inward eye which perceives the truth of what Krishna is pointing towards. In Buddhism, this is called the buddha-field, where one's energy attains a calmness, a bliss, a feeling of meaning, and starts dropping all that is unnecessary, starts dropping its conditioning. Then you can look at life with the eyes of beauty, with the eyes of infinite possibility, understanding that you are to attain an inward energy of greatness. And then everything else in your life becomes great.

Dis-identify from Ego

Usually, we identify with our ego. People like to feel great through the ego, they like to feel important through the ego. But Krishna's way is completely different. He's taking Arjun back to innocence, he is making him completely drop the ego. Arjun enters the meditative state. And in that meditative state, his discontentment disappears. His idea of worldly success and failure disappears. He realizes that true happiness is a miracle that is brought out by one's inward, inspired energy. When you understand the sacred inspired quality of existence, then your heart starts joining in its blissful flow. Then you forget about the non-essential.

Usually, our mind keeps roaming around the non-essential aspects of life. But Arjun starts seeing with a deeper insight. Once he acquires the message of Krishna's words, then he becomes happy *as he is*. Through the awakening of his spiritual and mental faculties, Arjun starts awakening to happiness. Happiness is not a state of something *happening*. It is a state of our heart awakening, our mind awakening. Through that, happiness is attained. And that is the whole idea of the Gita. Through that, love is also attained; through that, great ability and capability is also awakened. Our highest potential is never attained without understanding the spiritual meaning of life.

The Divine Stream of Consciousness

The divine stream of consciousness that Krishna is imbuing in Arjun and making him realize within his heart, is what eventually gives Arjun the courage to drop his misgivings, his doubts and miseries. And once he does that, he goes beyond his disillusionment and disappointment: his apprehension of what will happen if he fights the war, his apprehension about killing others, and so on. He becomes more conscious. And through that consciousness comes about the higher aspect of his being. He becomes more inwardly peaceful, more meditative, more mentally relaxed and silent. And the more and more silent he becomes inwardly, the more does his ability to fulfil his true nature as a warrior starts coming about. He becomes open, he frees his mind. He becomes receptive to the higher truth of the universe. And through that, he attains a higher state of functioning, a higher state of being.

Arjun had previously closed his mind to possibilities. He had a tunnel-vision. He was looking through what his mental impulses told him: that it is wrong to fight, that his energy should not be used as a force of destruction, and so on. Morally, that may seem right, but what Arjun was doing was that he was using these arguments to support his ego. His ego was not willing to look into the higher aspect of the struggle of justice that India's ancient war of the Mahabharat was all about. And Arjun's fundamental role in it, as a fighter for justice, was very important in the Mahabharat. Therefore, he could not just shirk his duty. By shirking his duty, he is shirking the ultimate value of his own life, his own existence.

Eventually, Arjun has to go past his own pain. He has to go past his own destructive feelings. And that is the way we also must function within the world.

Often we have to come out of our own comfort zone, our mental grooves, our ideas of what is right and what is wrong. We have to look deeper into life, not just intellectualize everything. And then we can function with the completeness of our energy. And functioning with the completeness of our energy is really what takes us beyond being miserable, what takes us beyond being unhappy, because then our energy can flow.

Life is comprised of various energies. We are creatures of a bio-energy. But there's a spiritual or mystical energy within us also. Within this bio-energy, this biology of ours, is the mystic truth of ourselves. And from that mystic truth come about all the true values of life.

If within your mystical self, you are flowing, then your psychology and physiology start getting strengthened, start flowing with renewed inspiration. Because now, your innermost nature, your ultimate nature of spiritual truth has been awakened and inspired. You have witnessed your higher self, you are no longer blind to the higher nature of yourself. And Krishna's Bhagavad Gita is all about awakening Arjun to his own higher, inspired self. Seeing that, Arjun is able to discover within himself that god is diffused within him, god exists within every pore of his being. And god exists within every pore of the universe. In that way, Indian religions are very different from several other world religions: they assert the primacy of the sacred element *within and not just outside* our material existence.

Within Every Atom

The aspect of Krishna is not considered to be separate from the universe. Krishna, or Narayan, pervades the universe. Within every molecule is his essence. Within every atom is his consciousness, his awareness. It just has to be awakened. So, it's a very interesting aspect about Hindu philosophy or Sanatan Dharma, that within the innermost truth of the microcosm resides the highest truth of the macrocosm, the greater, the absolute. We simply have to understand that the energy that is throbbing in the largest star is also throbbing within us.

Realizing inspired self-energy is the root secret of going past our fears. Of going past all darkness, of filling ourselves with the essence of the life divine, of finding great freedom of mind-body-spirit, of knowing that our nature is pure consciousness, pure inspired bliss. And that way, we attain a great luminous aspect of ourselves. We go past identifying ourselves with the structure of body and mind. We identify ourselves with that formless, vast, unlimited, unbounded self which Krishna proclaims himself to be. And that is the abode of eternal bliss, eternal power, eternal stillness, eternal peace. This takes us towards true, fearless, and successful living.

CHAPTER-2

The Soul

The great ancient sage of India, Dattatreya Rishi, says in his Avadhut Gita, 'The highest knowledge is that I am pure Soul: formless, pervasive, indestructible, luminous, pure intelligence!'

And this is one of the key teachings within the Bhagavad Gita also. One of the most significant things that Krishna is conveying to Arjun is to move *from body-consciousness to soul-consciousness*, to begin understanding that the soul is the luminous part of ourselves. And that without touching that luminous part of ourselves while we are alive, we can never really come to an understanding of what real happiness, real fearlessness, and real blissfulness in life itself means. Move towards soul-consciousness, and you automatically move towards becoming more capable to deal with tough times and emerge victorious.

The Avadhut Gita says: 'The soul is supreme truth. It cannot be harmed. It is completely free. Realize that it is changeless and infinite! The soul is beyond sorrow. Be happy by being detached from material things, and knowing yourself as pure soul.' This view is also supported by the great boy sage of ancient India, Ashtavakra Rishi, in his famous Ashtavakra Gita (a distilled masterpiece of the highest Vedic wisdom). The mystic philosophy of Advaita Vedanta (as taught by the great Adi Shankaracharya and others) teaches the oneness of the Supreme or *Paramatman* to the individual human being or individual soul, the *Jivatman*.

Knowing the Soul

The entire effort of man in the material world is meaningless unless he is also able to perceive the soul, or his *essential being,* as the true light of himself. Otherwise he leads only a bodily existence. And this is what Krishna is telling Arjun: he teaches him to look at the soul from the perspective that *it is not born nor does it die in the way that we do at the material level.* He also teaches that only in understanding yourself as a part of the super-soul or Supreme of the universe can you feel content in life. Otherwise, man is constantly buffeted between sorrow and joy; he is not established within the most essential part of him—that is the *spirit of things,* the lamp or light of being (seeing this light, the fear of death goes).

A Soulful Perspective

The body-mind becomes luminous with the understanding that it is a temple within which the light of the Divine has descended in the form of the soul. With this perspective, the whole manner of looking at life undergoes a change. You suddenly start feeling happy. You suddenly start feeling spiritually blissful, energized! And that is exactly what happens to Arjun: he moves from body-consciousness to soul-consciousness.

And remember this: *soul* is not to be looked at as a material thing, or as *a 'thing'* at all! Rather it is *the subtle essence of life*. It is not an object but is rather a quality, an essence. It is like the sweet scent of a flower: that scent cannot be said to be a *real thing or object having a particular origin, but exists nonetheless*. It is the *essence* of the flower. The same can be said of the soul. And there is no conflict between the body and the soul: when the soul is manifested in matter, it brings the energy of intelligence to that matter. It suffuses it with consciousness.

But there is one simple problem: man's ego forgets this essential spirit.

Our awareness is not on this essential spirit, and hence, we forget what it truly means. What it truly means is to achieve a completeness of spiritual life.

The whole essence of living spiritually is to feel the beauty of all existence but not by dreaming and desiring material things. It is about resting in the consciousness that you belong to a greater essence. That while you walk on the Earth and while you are in the body functioning through your senses, the master of it all is a luminous thing which has been called the soul. In Hinduism it has been called the *atman* (and the greater manifestation or the procreating entity of *atman* is the paramatman or super-soul, the Supreme Reality).

The Gita's View: Roots

The position of the Gita is clear: without moving from body-consciousness to soul-consciousness, life is lived in chaos. No matter what we achieve, we would feel that the roots are missing. Understand this: the roots of the tree are the most essential thing. They are hidden under the soil, but essentially they are responsible for the flower and the fruit which the tree is going to give. Without it there is nothing. Krishna is telling Arjun that his whole perception of reality is distorted. He's bringing him back to the path of understanding the meditative state; and the meditative state leads to identification with the deepest part or *roots* of ourselves, which can be called the soul. And once we taste that feeling of the soul through the meditative state and through the act of devotion or through the essence of love, then we feel that it is the divine bursting forth with dynamism everywhere! In that manner, we feel a great fulfilment in our being. Else, man is completely dull, man cannot see that it is the same truth of the universe expressing itself in billions of forms.

To 'see' or perceive the soul means understanding that all manifested material life is an expression of something more subtle. It is part of something which is of the higher dimension, and that higher dimension is *hidden* within us. Once you reconcile with this truth—that the higher dimension is also hidden within you—you automatically rejoice in life! The whole vibe of your living, changes. You start becoming freer in your mind.

The Perception of the Soul

The perception of the soul is the beginning of the freedom of the mind. It is the beginning of creativity. Without it, we go into a state where we are not really able to become spiritually stronger and dig deeper, because we are simply being buffeted by a situation where all sorts of childish worries and miseries are constantly creating trouble for us.

Man fears suffering. But the whole science of the soul is that when you understand yourself to be part of the greater reality or joined to the greater reality (the subtle essence of 'spirit'), then nothing makes you afraid! Because then you feel infinite. Then you feel as if the whole of creation is yours. And that you belong to it, and it belongs to you! So this feeling is of the interior; this essence of understanding comes when the misconceptions about life start dropping off.

Leave Misconceptions Behind

Through the Bhagavad Gita, Krishna is making Arjun drop all misconceptions about life. Arjun has many questions: for example, he wants to know what happens after death. Krishna is saying that in an ultimate sense, *all is death or nothing is death:* it is all part of the same cosmic reality, established in the super-soul or paramatman behind all things. And while it looks like everything is changing within the manifest cosmos, in fact, everything is the same because it's part of the same cycle. It's tremendously vast, but it's also tremendously simple to understand for the heart which has seen the soul. In seeing *the dimension of the spirit* is all human fulfilment. Otherwise there's no human fulfilment.

Man is always thinking of 'higher achievement'. Man is scarcely ever thinking of enlightenment! It is when we quest for enlightenment itself that we attain it. Once, Buddha was asked this: 'Why don't more people attain enlightenment?' He simply asked another question in return: 'How many people actually crave enlightenment?' The answer is obvious: very, very few! People are more content in different sorts of material miseries and in different types of drives towards more and more material pleasures/enjoyments/entertainments. There is scarcely a moment where they can leave their entertainments, where they can leave their worries and their preoccupations, and come back to a situation where they unify in a deep inner silence with that which is the essence of themselves: the soul.

The Super-Soul

As mentioned, according to Indian wisdom, the essence of the cosmos is the super-soul, that which we can call paramatman. Through this mystic realization of the vaster spirit of things, all things fall into order. Everything becomes spiritualized!

Yes, it may look irrational to our modern sensibility to look at life in this way, but if we look at all people of true inspiration or the greatest human beings who walked the planet (eg. Buddha, Archimedes, Ramanujan, Albert Einstein, etc.), we'll find the deep touch of this mystical element within them! They had this very *soulful* element in their lives. You can look at Bach or Mozart in the West, or the great musicians from the Indian classical tradition, or the great painters, the great inventors: they all had this mystic flight of vision! It is called *inspiration, but it is really a soulful way of living.* That is why when somebody gives a very good artistic performance we say it's a 'soulful' performance: implying that there's something beyond the person's personality which comes into it.

This is the touch which a great poet like Rabindranath Tagore had, this is the touch which William Shakespeare had. All good things on the human plane have some inspiration of the beyond, and that is because the people who have channellized those energies have felt the action of the soul more than their limited individual mind.

They have been able to merge their minds in the infinite. And through that mental merging with the infinite has come about something which is not futile and a waste of time, but rather has been of *great value* for all of society. And that is what a *yogi* means, that is what a sage means. This is precisely what Krishna is trying to tell Arjun—that by doing your work in a *spiritually inspired* state you automatically attain real yoga. You do not have to *attain* anything else, all will be spontaneously attained. And this is a very good template for leaders, and for the growth of every human being, in every situation. It is a multi-dimensional view of existence. It is a view of looking at life in a spiritual attitude. But at the same time it is an inspirational attitude, and inspiration is the basis of all passion in any task you want to carry out. You can look at any team in an organization: if it is charged with something soulful, with some inspiration which is beyond just the material goal (a higher calling or purpose), you'd find that the team becomes much able in its ability to accomplish the task. And the leader leading the team acquires a different kind of charisma.

The Greater Reality

Hence, it all really begins from understanding that we are part of a very great reality. And that this great existence is not really to be approached through just a very 'rational' or 'logical' approach, because that can be very limiting. The real genius of higher perception and mystic realization happens when we move beyond just material descriptions. Moving beyond these, we find that there is something *beyond matter* which eventually brings contentment (because mere matter cannot bring ultimate contentment)! That is the voice of the soul, that is the voice of the Divine speaking within us. And that is what Arjun experiences through the Gita. In intuitive flashes, guided by Lord Krishna, Arjun is able to go deep within himself and realize that he is just a part of that super-soul which is governing all things! And so doing, he finds his inner peace. He finds the silence of the heart. And he finds also that *connection* with the fullness of life which was missing in his moments of anxiety.

Arjun had been cut away from life's essence; through the Gita, he has become receptive, he has become dynamic. He starts allowing the energy of the Greater to occupy the space within his heart. And so doing, he has entered a deep state of meditation. And while it looks like Arjun was previously *compassionate*—thinking about his fellow warriors, his friends, and his foes—it is only now that his compassion has come to a maximum. Because he knows that the true act of compassion is to *act with a clear consciousness*. Where there is clear consciousness, the right thing will be done! And that is essentially true compassion. So he is also acting out of empathy. It's not like he's in a very egoistic state as a warrior: he is in fact in an evolved state.

Evolving

Real evolution means an unblocking of consciousness. Unblocking of consciousness has really got to do with removing those blockages that prevent us from seeing the light of the soul within ourselves. And these blockages are within our own selves, these blockages are just *the way of seeing or perceiving*. These psychological and emotional blockages are primarily caused by one thing: thinking that our enjoyment of life lies in material things.

The other way of looking at life is to look at it in a centred manner: where you feel that your individual soul is only a witness to the working of the super-soul of the cosmos. In that manner, you attain a oneness with that infinity. You attain a oneness with that super-soul. And then you awaken to a new state of certainty, a new state of spiritual evolution and bliss!

All of life is about creating a reliable foundation from which you can enjoy life itself. It is ultimately not about *attaining* something. Attainment will happen in its own time, but the spiritual view is about finding a solid basis within which your intelligence is able to move freely. Within which your intelligence is able to realize its highest state. That is, according to the Gita's wisdom, the very basis of intelligence. The Gita is the science of the soul, and the science of the soul illumines you so much from within that it destroys your ego! It makes you pay attention to the very basis and source of yourself. And so doing, you become intuitive.

Like Arjun, you become insightful. You become capable of finding your own dynamic approach to life. And you forget about all those nonsensical things which have been troubling you. You relax into your own presence, and you become full of a very potent energy which allows you to function to your maximum. And takes you not only to harmony, but also perhaps toward the state of enlightenment: a place of higher love, a place of higher energy, a place where you can fulfil your highest destiny.

CHAPTER - 3

It's All about Energy

In their essence, the Upanishads and the Gita are all about energy. For the 'warrior' on the battlefield of life, facing a tough situation, it is all a question of the amount of energy he or she is feeling which determines the course of their 'warriorhood' and the success of their lives. It is key to determining how we move towards fearless living.

All material creation in Hinduism is centred around the concept of higher energy, manifested as Nature herself: *Prakriti* or *Adishakti*. Therefore, realizing our higher energies within each moment is the key to the Hindu mystic viewpoint. The secret of all yoga is energization of consciousness *(chaitanya),* besides that of our material selves. The idea is to become full of the light of higher energy from within: the *tejomaya* or high-energy state. Krishna, as previously mentioned, is called *Yogeshwara*—the Lord of yoga—and as this ultimate master of yoga, he is taking Arjun to this high-energy state. Through the teachings of the Gita, Krishna energizes Arjun such that Arjun can face up to the challenge with joyful dynamism, and be the very best he can be.

Low Energy and High Energy

Now, all of us have low energy and high energy moments. That is natural: there will be dynamic moments or active moments, and there will also be passive moments. But the idea is to remain at peace in both kinds of moments. This is the fundamental essence of the ancient Hindu texts. Inner peace leads to outward poise, purposeful productivity, and a passion for progress even in the face of challenging situations!

Understand this core spiritual principle: no

matter if you are in the middle of an aggressive battle or if you are sitting in meditation, there is something deep within you that can be at peace! That is yours to decide upon: simply decide, 'No matter what, my inner peace will be undisturbed, undiminished!' This resolve and determination opens new vistas of courage and wisdom in your life, leading to resolution of problems you may have thought insurmountable! Life in the inner spiritual dimension must be a dance of the soul, unstrained, natural, passively peaceful. As if you are a pure witness to the goings-on of this vast cosmic play we call life. That is the spiritual attitude.

Inner Peace

This inner peace/silence/tranquillity is the bedrock of the Gita and its teachings. It is a question of the meditative energy you build within yourself which will tide you over all sorts of situations, both in your active life and in your passive moments. Remove the obstructions which you are feeling within. This will centre you, and enable you to attain silence deep within yourself.

The Upanishads say: 'When the mind is silent, it enters a world beyond itself, the Higher!' This is the very basis of Vedic knowledge, the heart of Hindu mystic truth.

Hence, the entire Vedic idea is to create a foundation of silent peacefulness deep within our being. Most of us do not feel inwardly at rest or centred: we are constantly moving from one mood to the other, one feeling or emotion to another feeling or emotion. And sometimes we just become deeply paralysed and incapable of dynamic action. Why is this? It is because we identify with the circumstances we are placed in, but the teaching of the Gita is extraordinary, because it says that nothing can take away that inner peace even if all around you there is destruction.

The Test of the Warrior

The test of the true warrior, in any battle of life, is that he keeps his mind afloat in the spiritual mode. He does what needs to be done when it needs to be done. True maturity of the warrior means that he or she is not invested in any sort of ego trip (*mithya-abhimana* or false egoism) or fear (*bhaya*). Both aspects are to be treated almost as the same, equal. Then their power over you, their power over your mind, gets taken away. Then you become the master who can guide the proverbial 'chariot' (Krishna is Arjun's charioteer during the Gita), instead of just being buffeted by life's waves.

Hence, the appropriate attitude which the Gita professes for the warrior (and in fact for every person) has got nothing to do with religious scriptures as such. It has more to do with an attitude towards life itself. It has got to do with your inner understanding. It has got to do with a situation where your energy within is never tired.

Emotional Well-Being

Most of us feel tired because of the anxious emotions we have at any particular moment: if it is an emotion which makes us feel low in the mind, we become drained of energy. Similarly, Arjun is drained of energy on the battlefield. But as the Gita is expounded to him by the Lord, he becomes filled with a renewed energy. The distance between his inner consciousness and his action becomes bridged, becomes one. And then he becomes truly dynamic!

So, the secret is to listen deeply to the voice of the Greater, as Arjun did, and be attentive to that deepest part of yourself which remains undisturbed no matter what is happening on the surface. Be identified with the sea and not with the waves! Be in an inner state such that ideas and circumstances do not have the power to drain you of energy. Be in an inner attitude that at any point you are able to tap into that divine feeling, that inner music, which is your essence. The Gita is basically musical: it is a song of the divine and its whole teaching is to fall into tune with the divine rhythm that is being played out in the cosmos.

Through such an inner attitude, you become a great receptacle of energy. You become much stronger than you ever thought you were! Because you mentally flow spontaneously with the ideation of something *larger* than yourself. But remember, it is not to be an enforced attitude: it is simply a question of being in rhythm. Remove the toxins of negative thought, remove the toxins of myriad negative feelings! And thereby attain that deeply cleansed situation where all comparisons have been dropped, all tensions have been released, all hostile thoughts have been dissolved, all inner frustrations removed. Move towards serenity.

This is the whole crux of the matter: that deep down it is your responsibility to create your own state of consciousness! Nothing can disturb it: it is ever free of all outer things. Be it honour and dishonour, respect and disrespect, glory of position, riches, recognition—these are things which are constantly changing in the cycle of the world and in the cycle of life. But if you listen to the deepest voice of consciousness—that of the divine element which exists within yourself—then you find that you have a 'kingdom' of great calm within yourself. It is the internal 'kingdom' of meditative energy. Attaining meditative energy brings courage, brings steadiness of heart and mind. And steadiness of heart and mind are the bedrock of the Gita's teaching.

The Mind

It's all essentially about how the mind functions: whether it is easily disturbed, or whether the energy of it is able to flow without feeling disturbed. And that is essentially a choice. The basic tendency of human beings is to get lost in the feelings and emotions they undergo: these could be feelings of happiness, or feelings of sorrow. But the Gita says that we are not to become *lost* in these feelings. Step out and be a witness to the feelings. Let the river flow, let the movie of life carry on as it is: observe them with a detached mind. Feel that you are much deeper! And through this ideation of feeling deeper, you attain an extraordinary new beginning. Where you are ever fresh, where you are ever renewed and revitalized at the deepest essence of yourself. That is the secret of real energy.

Positive energy creation means to not be a slave to the troublesome thoughts that absorb you. In the Gita, Arjun has become a slave to the feelings and frustrations that are haunting him. He's feeling a deep sense of regret, and he's identifying with that. In itself the feeling of regret is not wrong, *evil*, but to *identify* with it is wrong because it breeds inaction.

And in the fight for justice which Arjun has undertaken, he is becoming incapable of really good action. The better part of him is ceasing to come into play. Krishna is simply encouraging the best parts of Arjun to come into play, into the battle. Then only will there be a creation of justice for society—for Arjun is expected to help win the war against the doers of injustice (Duryodhan and the Kauravs). And then only will there be a creation of bliss for all.

Detachment

The correct psycho-spiritual attitude is of being slightly detached. In a very calm manner, be detached from whatever you are doing. For in that manner alone do we become more efficient at what we do: the archer becomes a better archer, the swordsman becomes a better swordsman, and so on. And so doing, through this smooth mentally detached flow, you are better able to transcend tough times.

Remember this: the example and metaphor of the 'warrior' is just a way of explaining a broader concept for successful and fearless living. What is *truly* important is the state of consciousness that it's seeking to signify. If that state of consciousness is one of peace and joy, all that comes out of it as action within the world also manifests itself joyfully and energetically! You come to a realization of yourself and you are able to effortlessly release your *higher* potentiality. Else, you remain limited by your lower self, which is constantly fearful, afraid, and frustrated at *what may happen or may not happen.*

The Gita's Practicality

In our everyday situations this principle becomes very important. And the Gita is immensely practical. The everyday situation could be anything: starting a new business, a new job, a new relationship. The point is: you have to simply get your baser feelings out of the way. Then only will the lamp be kindled within your heart. And then only can you become a great fount of courage, not only for yourself, but as an example to the world. Krishna again and again tells Arjun that he must be a good example to the world, not just feeling good within himself by doing his duty in life, but also being a good example for those he lives with, works with, and so on.

The Gita is alchemical: it is about turning negative energy into positive energy. That is the secret of alchemy. And that is what essentially the

Gita teaches. Negative energy can be transmuted and changed into positive energy, provided you do not get clouded and stupefied by the circumstances which you face in life. Life can be very complicated but also very simple: look at it as a great cosmic *harmony* which is moving so awesomely! And the entire idea is to proceed in a *harmonious* way. When you are in tandem with that cosmic harmony echoing deep within yourself, then you find that *whatever you do* has great energy. Else, whatever you do is not going to be energetic. It is only going to be half-hearted. And being half-hearted is the saddest thing in life, because it does not give you the opportunity to explore your potential to the maximum. Drop the feeling of lacklustre energy, and be luminous in your effort! This is a very significant part of what Krishna is telling Arjun. And in that manner, he is bringing about an immense growth of all that is good within Arjun's energy! It is a great example for all of us to follow in our practical lives.

All Is Divine

The ancient Vedic and Hindu mystical view of the universe was that we are to recognize *the whole world* as being filled with the *divine (divya)*. And that as citizens of the universe, we too can enjoy *the divine blissfulness* of all things! In fact, that is what we are here for. It is our right! Seeing this, realizing it, we are able to proceed towards a fearless and joyful state of being. And that makes us able to overcome tough times with great strength, great resilience, great fearlessness, and vigour of consciousness.

The whole idea of yoga, in Hinduism, is this internal union with the Divine, deep within our consciousness. In fact, the basis of India's highest sacred texts, including the Vedas and the Upanishads, is that everything material is simply a medium for the divine and ultimate spiritual entity. In other words, you too, at the material level, are just really a receptacle, a container as it were, of a deep spiritual essence. You carry the divine within you. You carry an infinite reality within you. The Upanishads say: '*Aham Brahmasmi*', meaning 'I am the ultimate divine reality!' This very idea makes you feel unlimited, makes you feel fearless, makes you suddenly relax and realize that, even if the body is harmed, your most essential 'self' (soul or atman) is not harmed. You are part of a great infinity of being. Knowing this, you are able to pull the mind out of its fear. And pulling the mind out of its ideas of fear is the best thing you can do when it comes to crisis situations. This is a central tenet of Hindu mysticism.

Every citizen of the universe has the freedom—the individual freedom—to have this recognition of the blissful divineness of all things, in their own individual manner. This is the basis of dynamic living, the first step towards a truly courageous, successful, and cosmically realized life. This understanding allows us to look at life with the attitude that no matter what, we must be completely dynamic and forward-looking: that nothing can stop us from living our lives with joy deep within the core of our hearts and minds. This understanding of the divineness of all things is the essence of Hinduism's highest sacred texts, including the Bhagavad Gita.

Beyond Struggling

Ultimately, every being in the universe is struggling for existence. But every being also has a share in that cosmic intelligence which is the light behind the cosmos. This light of consciousness can be shared equally, no matter what one's individual circumstances, position, or present situation in life. This understanding is the means to supreme cosmic bliss *(brahmananda)* and spiritual satisfaction *(atma tripti)*.

It implies that we are very much a part of a great divine intelligence that powers the universe, and are never separate from it. (This is also the secret of why the ancient Vedas of India gave symbolical meaning to the elements, eg. 'Agni' the intelligence behind the principle of fire, 'Varuna' that of water, and so on.) All things are part and parcel of a cosmic consciousness, and feeling connected to it has the power of empowering us during life's greatest challenges.

Through Krishna's wondrous exposition of the Gita, Arjun starts recognizing the divine element within all things, and his eyes fill with wondrous joy with that understanding! He is able to overcome the tough situation, and that is how we must be too. This understanding of perceiving the divine within all things gives us the inner wisdom and power to deal with tough times of all kinds, on all fronts: professional, personal, emotional, and so on.

Beyond 'Matter'

It is the view of the Upanishads, the Gita, and of the ancient mystics: that you are *not* to look at yourself as only being comprised of matter (Vedanta says, 'To the truly wise, the material and matter are in reality nothing but an appearance'). When you decide to dis-identify yourself as a creature of mere matter, then only do you begin attaining a richness that is spiritual, a richness that reminds you that no matter what, you can always find that element of the divine which can make your whole life into a great jubilation. You perceive yourself as being mind-body-spirit and not just mind-body. And then you suddenly begin seeing beyond all limitations, and perceiving the Infinite, the divine dimension! And that brings great freedom, happiness, and self-power, that are intrinsic parts of your *natural divine nature* because they are parts of the sacred infinite (Vedanta supports this: 'The Infinite, free and limitless, joyful and serene, is your *true and divine nature.*')!

Indeed, just as in the Gita we see how Arjun is able to glimpse into the infinite dimension and find his spiritual freedom (along with his highest ability to fight dynamically as a warrior), so too must we remember that we are part of a great divine fabric. And that it exists deep within us, waiting to express itself and make us transcend all challenges. All we essentially need to do is remember this sacred natural state or larger aspect within!

This is key to realizing the highest yoga, the

brahma-yoga: seeing yourself and the entire cosmos *(vishwa)* as part of an endless divinity.

Now, for the first time you realize that true evolution is not just psychological or physical evolution; it is about finding the highest values within the universe. And those values are essentially mystical and spiritual values. They are values which can help all the citizens of the cosmos make their lives full of the unfolding of self-potential, full of fearlessness and love, and a passion for living.

The ancient mystical view of the universe is essentially that of feeling this divine ideation, and suffusing your entire consciousness with it. Through this very act comes about a realization of that which is *greater* than us, an expansion of our consciousness into what the spiritual reality of the universe really is.

Mystical Realization

No matter what science says, the real taste of freedom in life can only be gifted to us through mystical realization. No amount of scientific knowing can free us within. At the most, it can expand our horizons. But to truly love, cherish, and delight in the ecstasy of life itself requires us to open our eyes unto the greater vistas of the spiritual and divine dimensions of the universe. So it all begins by continuously flowing and continuously evolving to a state where you wonder at the great mystery of life itself.

The universe is a mystery, the cosmos is a mystery, but even greater than that is the mystery of its very *being there*! Man has not been able to even come close to answering *why* the universe exists, why we ourselves exist. And while there may not be an ultimate answer to this, there is a dimension where you can feel it: as a gentle delight in your heart, a freedom and opening of the mind. So that is the mystical element, that is the spiritual element. It is not about going to a house of worship, but instead about treating the *entirety* of the universe itself as a house of worship within which we can dance our divine dance. In fact, in Hinduism, the cosmos itself is represented as a product of dance and rhythm: emphasized by the iconic dancing Lord Shiva or Natraj, the one who keeps bringing existence towards annihilation so that once again things can be born anew.

Within this wondrous universe, we are to delight in all the gifts of life that it has granted us. And this realization is freely accessible to us as individuals. But the whole problem with us human beings is that we seldom value that which is freely given! If only we can begin to appreciate the spiritually delightful dimension, we would find that we need not be disheartened: because that which we most deeply seek is in the realm of the *intangible*. It is always in the realm of *consciousness*, in that which is beyond the material. Yes, material means are essential and almost mandatory to live a good life. But once that is secure, it is up to us to create a great urgency of energy in the direction of being enlightened. That means moving towards answers about what it spiritually means to be placed in this universe, in this very particular time and place we have been placed in! That is real appreciation of life. That is real appreciation of the mystic dimension.

A Crisis of Consciousness

Now, the greatest crisis on our Earth is, fundamentally, not one of material wants but in fact a crisis of consciousness. And that has led to all sorts of violence, all sorts of destruction. All things begin with consciousness. And to understand the universal dimensions, all it requires is a change in consciousness whereby you can understand the wholeness of things. It begins by understanding that deep down within you—at a very subconscious level—is a great longing to want to understand the deeper cosmic dimensions, to feel one with them. And where there is this feeling of oneness, all things come into a great flow. All things come into a great integration of energy. So it is not *secondary* to our lives, it is a *primary* requirement for having quality in life.

The quality of our mortal lives actually depends on the timeless and immortal dimension that our consciousness can inwardly travel to. Because only then can the mind wonder about how much love and how much creativity it must have taken for the divine to build this fathomless, endless, and delightful cosmos that is our home! Sooner or later, man has to begin to think that this whole cosmos is home, and not just the Earth. Because that feeling itself is one of the most transformative things.

The primacy of the divine becomes Arjun's prime realization, through the teachings of Krishna's Gita.

Taking the first step of understanding the divine dynamism within the universal dimension of things, Arjun moves towards fearless action and success.

CHAPTER - 5

Five Secrets of Hinduism

The Gita and Hinduism contain the deepest, most insightful secrets for human beings to attain their best selves. The Gita is a sermon which tells us how to act in the here and now, without anxiety, without fear, with absolute clarity. And to understand these things, five key points are essential:

a. The first aspect which we have to look into, is that the Gita is primarily a text on the soul or atma. It leads us not only towards God-consciousness but towards *atma gyaana*: knowledge of the innermost self. Krishna is reminding Arjun again and again to know the self, to know his deepest self. And through atma gyaana happens *brahma gyaana* or knowing the ultimate cosmic reality. The means to atma gyaana is *atma samarpan:* surrendering before the ultimate reality that Krishna represents (alternatively, *atma nivedan:* dedication of one's being to the higher principle). And through that, we attain what is called atma tripti or resting contented within the soul. Till you rest contented within your own soul, there is no contentment in the world. Till you are established within your deepest self in the state of *atma nishtha* (faith in your innermost reality), you will go on in a state of anxiety. Let go of all that, and you attain the true nobility of your innermost soulful being, your true reality.

b. The second point is purification of mind-body-spirit. This is called the process of *shuddhi*. There are various levels at which we are to purify ourselves. There is the level of the body, there is the level of the mind, and there is the level of the deeper consciousness, and ultimately, the level of our utmost inner atma or soul. The purification of the physical body-mind is *ghata shuddhi*. We can achieve that through the process of Raja Yoga which the Hindu sacred texts propound as one of the means to ultimate fulfilment. It encompasses *man shuddhi:* the purification of the mind. *Chitta shuddhi* implies purifying ourselves at the deepest psychological levels to become established in soulful, free, and happy living. By going deeper comes the realization of *chaitanya shuddhi* or timeless purity of our innermost consciousness which is deeper than superficial thoughts of the conditioned mind. All this leads us to perceive and realize the real abiding purity within ourselves, that of the soul or deepest part of the mind-body-spirit complex, the state of complete *atma shuddhi*. And this is essentially what Krishna keeps reminding Arjun of within the Gita. Being aware that we are to undergo purification at all these levels of being in order to attain the ultimate mystic state or *samadhi*, and the ultimate Krishna-consciousness, is the essence of the Gita.

c. The third thing is *dharma*. Through getting in touch with your innermost soul, you spontaneously attain dharma. Dharma means living rightly, living in a state of virtue, doing your duties with a state of virtue. But dharma comes about spontaneously when, at the level of soul, you have corrected yourself; when at the level of soul, your energy is flowing well. That is the key thing to know about dharma. There's no use in going about intellectual ideologies about dharma. If at the level of consciousness and soul you are doing fine, then dharma comes about spontaneously through you, because your innermost being becomes full of wisdom, and that light of wisdom starts reflecting in your activities. It's like they say in Vedanta: the light of the moon reflects slightly differently in various lakes and various puddles, but the light is the same. When you are luminous within your consciousness and within your soul-realization, then no matter what activity you do, what aspect of your life you choose, the reflection of that wisdom will happen.

d. This leads us to the fourth secret: the idea of becoming determined, full of conviction, full of courage, that which is called the state of decisive bravery or *nishchaya*. The state where you are completely *determined* to do that which you have to do. Arjun had become very hopeless. He had lost his sense of determination. And without the sense of determination, neither material nor spiritual success in life can be achieved. This is what Krishna is constantly reminding Arjun about. Ultimately, Arjun comes to the state of *nishchaya vritti*, the state of being where he has steadfast and steady conviction, self-confidence, hope in himself. And through that, he attains dynamism in action, dynamism in thought, dynamism in the way he looks at the world. And that creates success in the world. When you don't have conviction, how can others believe in you? And that is what Krishna tells Arjun. He says that Arjun is setting such a bad example. He reminds Arjun to pull himself up, pick up his bow and fight. And through the state of self-determination, Arjun picks up his bow called *Gandiva* and he begins fighting the fight as he's meant to.

e. The fifth secret is really the idea of holistic living: to become a *Purna Yogi*, to become a complete yogi, one who knows all the four aspects of yoga which Krishna talks about. Living a life in a state of *Purnata*, completeness, holistically, realizing that which is said in the Upanishads: '*Om Purnamadah Purnamidam, Purnaat purnamudachyate, Purnasya purnamaadaaya, purnamevaavashishṣyate, Oṁ Shāntiḥ, Shāntiḥ, Shāntiḥ.*' This implies that all things are part and parcel of a cosmic wholeness. The idea is that within the microcosm, within the individual component, the highest is also hidden like a seed. And this is something which is not just mystically true. It's scientifically true also. With the idea of the Mandelbrot set and fractals, it's been demonstrated in mathematics that the *smallest also carries part of the largest. Within the atomic exists the cosmic. So within you resides cosmic power, the infinite power.* And through that, you come to a state of that which is described in Vedic knowledge, the realization of *Purno'ham*, that 'I am whole, full, complete: I am *Ashesha* or limitless, unbounded! I am the nature of *Brahman*. I am the nature of the ultimate entity.' And through this, you attain true courage; through this, you attain true fearlessness, which is what happens to Arjun.

CHAPTER - 6

External to Internal

Before listening to the Bhagavad Gita, Arjun's mind was an extroverted mind. Being a warrior, his action was always outward. For the first time, Krishna is pointing him towards the inner state of being. And that is the ultimate spiritual journey. We have to go from the external to the internal. When the internal is going proper, other things can go proper in the external world. Without rectifying the internal state of being, how can the external things be of any consequence? They have no meaning. The whole secret of the Gita is that no matter what circumstances you're facing in the outer world, always refer back to your inner state. This determines the level at which you are able to cope with life's problems and challenges.

Now, the biggest problem with humanity is that we've become too extroverted, we have stopped being introverted. What's happened is that every activity of ours is almost like a performance. Very few are those moments in the day when we are internally within ourselves. Our focus is on the outer world. Hence, our *atma shakti* or *atma bala*—the power of the internal soul or spirit—gets depleted. It's not energized. And the way to energize this soul, the spirit of man, is through attention, through consciousness of that which is *within* you. That is what Krishna is teaching Arjun. But his lesson is *for us all*!

Don't just concentrate on outward things. Look inwardly, but look in a way that you have never looked before. Realize that within yourself, you are infinite. In the outer world, you are very finite, your abilities are very limited; there's only so much you can do. Even a great warrior like Arjun has his limitations on the battlefield. But all of us have an innate infiniteness within us. This *akhanda,* ashesha, unbroken and limitless part of us is what Arjun understands through receiving the wisdom of Gita. So not only does he receive the wisdom from Krishna, he also receives the gift of bliss. Real happiness or real joy, contentment and bliss in life are only found if you venture within. In Vedanta, it is called the *akhanda ananda*: the non-broken state of bliss within us.

Inner Power

Outwardly, you might be distracted by pleasures, entertainments. They bring some momentary joy. But, the only real way to find yourself to the utmost is reaching towards that unknown inner power which is deep within you. There, you are powerful; there, you are completely in a dimension that is beyond all limiting circumstances.

Arjun, withinwards, feels like there's a great deal of darkness in his life. He feels powerless within himself. And then from within himself, Krishna strengthens him! Krishna strengthens Arjun not by giving him any great ideal or telling him to be perfect, or giving him any moral instruction. Because, in

Krishna's point of view, all those things are also egoistic: thinking we are doing some 'good' in the world, thinking we are doing something of value in the world. Those are all parts of the egoic being, those are all parts of the old identity of yourself, the external identity which has to be shed.

Realize your internal identity! And your internal identity is simply an instrument of the greater power. That is what Krishna is making Arjun realize. And then the reality of his own nature starts dawning on Arjun. And realizing the reality of his nature, he is able to rise up and fight the battle with all his strength, all his power, all his energy, with all the light within his being. Suddenly, it is like a divine light has been lit up in his internal self. And when the divine light gets lit up in the internal sphere of yourself, then what is there to fear in the outer dimensions? Then you are able to move into any outer dimension with a lot of ease. Your anxieties and worries have been taken care of.

Most of us don't accept or acknowledge or address our inward anxieties. Therefore, our outward actions always have the touch of that anxiety. We are not total in our energy when we are acting. Hence, we always feel something is holding us back, we always feel there is something more to do. Now, an enlightened person whose *buddhi* or mind has been freed of these limiting factors, of worries and so on, is suddenly unleashed to be able to do what it *needs to do* in the outer world.

Being Free

The whole concept of Indian spirituality and the deepest Hindu mysticism is *mukti* or *moksha*: becoming free. And the main thing is we have to free the mind, the buddhi, of the cage of anxiety and worry. Then only do we move towards dynamic action in the outer world, then only do we move towards anything of worth in the world.

The chaitanya or consciousness of the inward spirit has to dawn upon you. Then automatically, great peace, great flow, a great upsurge of effortless energy comes about in all your actions and all your relationships. Suddenly, you find that you're transformed even when you're working in the outer world; because your state of consciousness is transformed. Hence, the true power within you is able to function in a far more harmonious manner. So, your atma bala, your spiritual energy gets enhanced, and so does your *buddhi bala* or your *buddhi shakti* (the power of your consciousness, the power of your intellect).

And that is what happens to Arjun. His wavering thoughts are dropped. His mind comes into a harmonious flow. And through that harmonious flow, he is able to function like he is total in his energy, but also relaxed at the same time.

Yoga: Completeness of Effort

The thing about action in the world is that you need to be complete in your effort, no matter what you're doing—you might be working in a technology company, you might be a scientist, you might be an artist. All outer actions need energy. But that energy has to come from within you. And within yourself, you have to light the lamp of true yogic or meditative harmony. That is what our real power is.

What is yoga? Yoga means you become united with the higher power. But that unison doesn't happen in the external world! That has to happen in your internal world.

In a way, Arjun and Krishna are speaking externally on the battlefield. But their *real meeting is the inward meeting,* where Arjun realizes that Krishna dwells within him as his utmost spirit, as his utmost god-consciousness, and so on. And then he's able to act in a way where he knows that, eventually, he is non-destructible. The body is destroyed, the material aspect of himself can be destroyed, but really, at his essence, he is indestructible! And that brings a sense of relaxation into Arjun's demeanour. Then, even as a warrior, he is able to function far more effectively.

You see, the whole problem with us in life is that we are on a see-saw: one moment up, one moment down. If we're given a position of power, we can become obsessed with its ego trip, its 'power trip'. On the other hand, if somebody ignores us, or if we are not finding enough traction from people in the work we do, we feel depressed. So, all our life-situations are determined by outward judgments of others. And on the judgments of others, we are making our own judgments about ourselves. This makes us incredibly weak. This makes us incredibly disempowered in the face of difficult circumstances.

The whole message of the Gita is attaining a

unity within yourself, a state of *ekatvam*. Through that state of ekatvam, you attain true action and empowered action or *kriya shakti*: the power to act according to the highest energy of yourself. This is the whole message of the *itihas* or the epics of India. It is the abiding message of the Ramayan and the Mahabharat, both. In the Ramayan, it happens through the persona of Ram. And in the Mahabharat, it happens principally through the persona of the Pandavas. They come to their own self-realization of their internal state of great inner power, peace, happiness, joy, enlightenment, and so on, knowing that these qualities are what manifest dynamic outward action.

The Internal Feeds the External

Internal qualities feed outer action. When you are internally calm, happy, non-egoistic, there is great dynamism in your outer action. You become a pure performer of action, realizing that you're not the ultimate *karta* or the doer, but that there is a greater universal action. When this realization happens, you get the power to come into a state of Kriya Yoga.

Kriya Yoga is the state of correct yogic action in life. It implies the ability to act freely, happily, selflessly, effortlessly. And when you act like that, you are able to move into the higher yoga, which is the *laya yoga*, where you, as an individual spirit, feel that you're at one with the supreme spirit!

Arjun eventually starts feeling that he's part and parcel of the greater transcendent super-soul which is Krishna, and through that, the goal or *lakshya* of life, that of spiritual liberation, is achieved. Then all the impurities, all the weaknesses of the mind start disappearing, and you find that you are able to soar up into greater flights of excellence. Inwardly, you become silent, you become peaceful, you become far more affirmative and feel good about yourself, because now, you realize that your self that you thought to be your true being is actually just a fraction of what you truly are.

You are part of this great truth, consciousness, and bliss: the *Sat-Chit-Ananda* that governs the entire universe, and which is personified by Krishna in the Bhagavad Gita. Knowing that, something within you deeply changes, and you're able to transform unhappiness or feelings of misery in your life, as Arjun is feeling, into moments of transcendence.

Then you move with greater dynamism, greater energy, greater bliss, and so on, which Arjun eventually does. And thereby, instead of becoming a force of destruction for his own self, Arjun starts becoming a creative force. His mind, instead of being destructive for himself—because it was destroying his valour, his courage—starts becoming an instrument to empower him. He is able to see that movement from darkness to light, that which the Upanishadic Rishis have said in these magical words: '*Om Asato Maa Sad-Gamaya, Tamaso Maa Jyotir-Gamaya, Mrtyor-Maa Amrtam Gamaya*: Lead me from falsehood to truth, from darkness to light, from death to deathlessness.' And that is what Krishna does to Arjun.

CHAPTER-7

Yoga Secrets

India's great modern mystic, Sri Aurobindo, referred to the Bhagavad Gita as a living text. And in fact, the Bhagavad Gita is not a sacred text like any other. It offers us lessons which are immensely practical in our present day-to-day lives. It is especially important as a summation of the core concepts of yoga philosophy that form the very foundation of Hinduism. The Bhagavad Gita talks about four yogas— *Gyaana Yoga*: the yoga of knowledge, *Karma Yoga*: the yoga of action, *Bhakti Yoga*: the yoga of devotion, and *Raja Yoga*: the yoga of meditative practices.

Now, yoga, by itself, means a union with the absolute reality, that which we may call god. It also means maintaining a completely tranquil, calm, serene state of mind in whatever activities and whatever path one is pursuing, because through that comes about this union with the divine element. And also through that comes about the feeling of Ananda: complete joy, complete happiness in whatever one does; in fact, not just ordinary *Ananda*, but *Ananta Ananda* or endless joy. And through feeling endless joy within, we meet that principle of the ocean of bliss, the ocean of happiness and joy itself which is *Ananda Sagara*. That is represented by Krishna in the Bhagavad Gita.

Yogas, as discussed in the Bhagavad Gita, go beyond any particular practice, but are eventually all about us feeling a quality of being, feeling a rhythm within ourselves which makes us transcend into spiritual relaxation, spiritual joy, spiritual dynamism. That is our birthright. That is our real self-potential. Hence, eventually, the Bhagavad Gita is about creating an inner state of cheerfulness amidst all circumstances. And that is what happens to Arjun when he hears the words of the Bhagavad Gita from Krishna's lotus lips. Inwardly, he starts feeling·bliss.

Yes, the outward action he has to perform is one of killing. He is a warrior. But his inward state of being becomes full of a different quality. And through this understanding of the yogas which Krishna expounds to him, Arjun is able to go into the very depths of the mystical search. He is able to heal himself inwardly.

The yogas are meant to heal us at the level of mind-body-spirit. They contain all the secrets which are needed for our well-being, our potential realization, our ability to be excellent in all spheres of life. We will discuss these yogas one by one.

Gyaana Yoga

Gyaana Yoga is the path of pure knowledge, the path of wisdom, the path of knowing who you really are. The secret of Gyaana Yoga within the Bhagavad Gita is surrender of the ego. When the ego is surrendered, only then the veil of true knowledge dawns on you. Else, all your knowledge is distorted by the idea of the ego, by the idea of your conditioning. The mind is so full of thoughts that the true light of the sun is not seen, because the mind is clouded.

Gyaana Yoga means clearing the clouds of thought, of anxiety, of self-created conditioning and society-created conditioning, so that the pure *jyoti* or light of spiritual knowledge dawns within oneself. And Gyaana Yoga is not only a part of the Vedic knowledge of India, it is part of the Tantric knowledge of India also. In Tantra, it is called *Gyaana Tantra*. The idea is that we enhance our true power of self-knowing, our true power of knowing the real energy of who we truly are in mind-body-spirit.

Arjun, on the battlefield, is thinking in terms of forms—who he'll kill, who he'll not kill. But Krishna explains to him that ultimately, all these different aspects, all these different personalities he's looking at as beings in the material sphere are simply spiritual entities who are absorbed back into Krishna.

So, Arjun's mind becomes completely free of the idea that he is going to be doing some sort of 'killing', because in actuality he is just an instrument of the lord, he's just an instrument of the universal will, who is carrying out his part in life. Even through the act of killing, he is only fulfilling a spiritual duty, because essentially, the beings he's killing are not comprised of matter alone. No! They are spiritual entities. They are pure soul. Every being is pure soul. In Gyaana Yoga, this idea is symbolized through the lotus existing within the mud. The lotus signifies the spiritual part of us. The mud signifies the material domain we have to exist within. But being like the lotus, you can spiritualize yourself even in the most difficult circumstances. Even on the battlefield of war, you have to look at things with a spiritual eye. Then you become dis-identified with the smaller material aspect of yourself, and identify instead with the higher aspect of yourself which is comprised of pure awareness, pure bliss, pure consciousness.

Karma Yoga

The second path of yoga is Karma Yoga. It implies the yoga of effortless action, where you are doing all that you need to do in the world, but there is something within you which is detached, there is something within you which does not think in terms of the results of your actions. The very act of doing those actions brings contentment, not thoughts about their results.

The secret of Karma Yoga is to be in a state of

flow within. You see, modern psychological theories that have come out from the West are telling us that too much anxiety about results disturbs the process of flow in any work. The people who are the highest achievers in any field—be it technology, be it business, be it art, and so on—are those people who flow into the work while they're doing it. They're not disturbed so much by the results of that work. They enjoy the process of work. They are absorbed. They give their entire energy into the very process of achieving excellence in what they are doing, within the present moment.

And when you do your best action in the present moment, it is bound to lead to better results in the future. So the secret of Karma Yoga is not to let the mind be in this constant rush of anxiety about what will happen as a consequence of your action or not. Relax into your being. Understand that you don't need to hurry. Understand that your greatest spiritual freedom is in investing all your energy in doing your work meditatively with great joy within your heart, with great light within your being. Then, that action which you do is sure to bring about excellence, is sure to bring about value-creation. And through that, you attain true success in life.

Raja Yoga

We come to the next yoga, called Raja Yoga. Now, Raja Yoga is synonymous with the *Ashtanga Yoga* or Eight-Limbed Yoga of Rishi Patanjali. But Krishna explains it as a system of deep meditation, where you try and attain a union with the highest through meditative practices, through the idea of *Kundalini Yoga*, through concentrated techniques such as *Vipassanā*: the watching of the breath, and so on. And the whole idea of Raja Yoga is one where you purify yourself through various Kriyas, through various actions. And these Kriyas can be of various sorts. They could be those which are described in *Hatha Yoga*, for example, *Pranayama*, yogic meditation, moving into Samadhi, and so on. It could also involve Kundalini practices, such as unlocking the primordial cosmic force which dwells within us, where you concentrate on the Chakras and ultimately, meet in a union with the divine within your highest spiritual centre: you go from the *Muladhara Chakra* or root chakra to the *Sahasrāra* or crown chakra, and you attain enlightenment.

In many ways, the practices of Raja Yoga also overlap with the practices of Buddhism, Jainism, and other spiritual philosophies. It is part of the oldest traditions of India. And the entire idea, the whole secret of Raja Yoga is that you act as a perfect witness. You do the *kriyas*, you do the actions towards meditative practice, but you maintain a detached view, you don't identify yourself with the mind, you keep your mind centred just like Buddha advised. That fills you with a coolness, where you become a watcher of the practices. You don't get lost in them. That creates a great centre of peace within you. And when you feel coolness within yourself, you become purified, you become fresh, your energy starts getting renewed by itself, you become a dynamo of energy.

Bhakti Yoga

The final yoga is what several have called the highest yoga: the attitude of the *Bhakta*, the attitude of the devotee who performs Bhakti Yoga, where, through devotion, you attain a union with the highest. And Bhakti Yoga is not unique to the Vedic knowledge which Krishna propagates. It is also very much a part and parcel of Tantra. For example, Shiva advises

Parvati to be in the attitude of spontaneous Bhakti Yoga, where spontaneously, through the eyes of love, through the attitude of oneness and *Prema* or higher love, you attain actual truth. So, it is a way of the heart. It is a way of heartfulness where you don't have to really search. You have to manifest love within your life.

The more and more love you manifest in your life, the greater and greater energy do you manifest within your life. And love can be a quality, not a feeling, you have towards an individual. Make love your very quality. You could be doing your work, you could be a carpenter, you could be a technician, you could be an artist, you could also be a warrior on the battlefield like Arjun. Yet, through love, you attain the ultimate cosmic principle, because the cosmic substratum is said to be comprised of love or *Prema* itself. That is the whole idea of the *Leela* or divine playfulness between Krishna and the *gopikas*, the milkmaids, Radha, and so on . . . especially Radha. Krishna's life has been described as a divine play of love. Its very basis is the secret of Bhakti Yoga. In this connection, it's worth mentioning a very mysterious, secret teaching of Krishna Bhakti that resonates with science: there are said to be nine principle gopikas dancing around Sri Krishna. It is an esoteric suggestion of the central sun of the solar system, around which the planets revolve! And when one looks at the whole concept of the *raas* leela, one would find remarkable features suggestive of a secret scientific cosmic code, hinting at the revolution of galaxies, at interstellar and cosmic concepts.

Eventually, Krishna's life's been described as a divine play of love. Understanding this, you start bringing more and more love, affection, empathy, compassion into your life. And through that, anxiety disappears. Through that, you become empowered. Through something as soft as love, you attain the highest power, the highest force, the highest strength to take on any problem in life.

CHAPTER - 8

The Bhagavad Gita
for Joyful Living

The Bhagavad Gita is ultimately a gospel for joyful living. It is not just a gospel about mystic philosophy, about warfare, about duty, responsibility, and so on. At its most intrinsic base lies the lesson of living joyfully, and hence of living fearlessly, successfully being able to go past tough times.

In Hinduism, our most subtle and root reality is considered the *Anandamaya-Kosha* (body of bliss, the final reality and quality of our soul). We are to manifest this quality of the soul's ananda—being filled with deep spiritual joy—within life's changing situations.

The Joy of All Things

All of nature and all of creation is bountiful in its joyful expression: there is so much opulence in the universe! That needs to be reflected in our own lives. And the eternal lesson which Krishna is teaching Arjun is that no matter what we are doing in life, there has to be an innate spirit of cheerfulness, of joy. Because only that will lead to a healthy, truly successful individual and a healthy, successful society. Without healthy individuals, a healthy society cannot exist.

Arjun is experiencing a mental illness: an illness of emotions. Krishna is bringing him out of this state. Doing so, Krishna is dynamizing the entire society that Arjun exists within because Arjun becomes a force of joyful energy, who begins doing his duty for justice in a manner which is powerful, compassionate, empathetic. Interested in strengthening the good roots of civilization, he takes forward the understanding of the divine element which exists within and behind all things.

The Gita, when looked at in a holistic perspective, teaches us self-respect. It teaches us inner dignity. And at the basis of self-respect and dignity, lies the ability to be joyful, no matter what happens on our material plane. The test of spirituality is in fact that of being able to have such joy and a sense of universal-hood: it is to delight in that which we have, and to make the most of that which we can create. The vision needs to be changed from the negative to the positive. The destruction of our old modes of thinking needs to be done, and that is what Krishna is doing within Arjun: he is destroying the old modes and structures of Arjun's mind, and in place of that comes about a fresh understanding, that *all is blessed,* all is joyful! That everything reflects the infinite bliss of the Absolute, the Creator, the Cosmic Consciousness.

Cheerfulness

Only to the fresh mind, only to the mind which is youthful, can come the idea of deep cheerfulness. Only to the mind which does not walk with the burden of thousands of years of conditioning, comes the miracle of living blissfully and truly joyously, and hence, dynamically! So the fight is simply to let go of the old structures of thought. And in its place will come a greater consciousness: that of simple yet incredibly deep spiritual joy.

The Bhagavad Gita is, first of all, about insights on what we can do within the world to the utmost of our capacities. But beyond that it is about insights into how the divine factor operates. And the divine factor is reflected in the natural richness of delight and joy which is bursting forth throughout the cosmos! The cosmos is a veritable treasure trove of joyful energy. It cannot come out of a depressed energy: it must have come out of a supremely blissful energy! And that is the energy which Krishna stands for. The whole phenomenon of life and death has got to do with our ability to understand that the more joyful we become, the more insightful we become. Because that leads to a massive trust, a deep-rooted genuineness and sincerity in living. Else, we are constantly in a state where nothing seems to satisfy us. And if we go through all of life hankering, complaining, and not stopping to see the changes in life (just as a change of seasons, just as a cyclical movement of things) then we are truly missing something. The problem is the mind's chatter—its very repetitive narrative—about how many ways we can be unhappy or sorrowful! That takes away the natural joy which is our birthright.

Being Adventurous

One of the most fundamental problems in man's psychology is the sense of boredom: a lack of excitement, a lack of true adventure unto unknown paths. Very few are those people who are real adventurers of consciousness! Krishna is making Arjun an adventurer of consciousness, and the greatest adventure has to be done with a spirit of joy! No mountain can be climbed if the climbers are dejected. So the first thing, the foundational thing, is to begin the journey with a sense of joy. Only then will we be able to climb the many mountains! Joy liberates us: it is the greatest freedom from fear.

What is cowardice? Cowardice begins with the state of constantly complaining! You'll see that the biggest cowards in life (simply look around you) are always complaining about something or the other! Whereas the most courageous people are those who are happy from within; who know what it is to be cheerful from within. They might not smile so much, they might not be so expressive. But there is something that abides in them which is part of the positive side of life. They can find bliss even in the midst of conflict! And Krishna is teaching Arjun to find this joy *even in the midst of his carrying out of the duties of warfare, as a warrior!*

Hence, it is all about being able to see the immense value in all things: to see the massive potential for joy that exists in life, and to move towards realizing that potential. If only we can have this inner attitude: that we have a great potential for joy! Let's actualize this potential.

But society and civilization usually seem to be moving to the other extreme: where it becomes not about realizing spiritual joy, but about realizing more and more material satisfaction. And that is in fact the wrong way of looking at things, because it does not create a wholeness of energy in society. A lot of negativities come out of that quest. For example, a person may grow in wealth, but without real values, he may also end up destroying happiness for a lot of others—it very often happens that way. And in the material sphere, this idea assumes drastic proportions, because with it comes the question of accumulation, power, domination, and so on. One example is that of modern warfare and how utterly destructive it is—because of dominance, of wanting to assert one's dominance over the other side.

War in the Mahabharat

Now, the war of the Mahabharat was entirely different: the whole battle within the Mahabharat was one for higher values and justice.

It was not about the Pandav brothers wanting to dominate the other side, but rather about setting an example and correcting the wrongs which existed in the prevailing power structure of their cousins the Kauravs, and within society. It was about destroying the whole negative atmosphere which has been created by the likes of Duryodhan and the Kauravs.

Sometimes, to eliminate the negative factor, it is important to stand up for what is right and fight! But ultimately, in the end, the whole circle of negativity and sorrow has to be broken by joy and mutual trust, regard, understanding. Only then is transformation possible. Otherwise, transformation is very transient and temporary.

The Illusion of Sorrow

The Bhagavad Gita's bold teaching is that you are not to be under the illusion that you have to be a slave of sorrow! Or that you have to be a slave of unhappiness. Look within: at any time, you can find the great spiritual smile of the Ultimate playing out within the deepest core of your being. Seek within: you can find that inner smile, you can find that inner joy. It is what is priceless in life. Everything else in life goes: it is temporary. But that which is eternal has the quality of a great freedom of joy. That is the essential spirituality which we must be concerned with. All else is mere philosophizing, and philosophizing does not really give us that taste of enlightened living which the simple act of perceiving our innate joy gives us.

And the beauty of Krishna is that he is an embodiment of pure joy even in his everyday life. Krishna was known for radiating such a luminosity of joy that people used to be electrified by it! So, from his words in the Gita and from his own *being* we can have that insight about joy. His very presence, his smile, radiates joy. For us, the lesson or the idea is to be deeply serene and joyful in our inward smile, and let it radiate unto all those we come into contact with. That way, the individual becomes a true leader, a conveyor of inspiration to others. That way, you are able to remove the anguish from people's minds along with your own. So you become a force of good without really *doing* anything, simply by being more joyful and radiating it to others! The beauty is that you are enhancing your own potential-realization as a result of acting joyfully within the world. It's all a question of believing that you *can* be joyful: that is what true *faith* is. That is what pure trust is. It's not about just being a seeker of truth. *Be a seeker of joy,* and you will be filled with that *spirit of cheerfulness.* You will see that all boundaries and barriers start melting before your eyes, that you are able to accomplish more, that you're able to get rid of the anxiety or hardness in your heart, the anguish or aggressiveness in your heart, and become totally open to the universe. This very sense of openness will create and redouble more and more joy within you. You become a dynamo of that quality, and so doing, nothing can distress you anymore.

Beyond Psychology

The whole question of mental distress in life cannot really be addressed by psychoanalysis or psychotherapy alone. Rather, it is a question of the spiritual revolution in your heart and mind. And the single most revolutionary thing you can do as far as the mystical dimension goes, is to see your 'real face' or true nature—which is one of pure joy! The nature of the soul has been described as being that of utter joy. So reflect that nature of the soul in your everyday living.

In the Gita, Krishna is taking us far beyond psychology. Krishna is taking us to that realm where the essential learnings of mankind can be found. The most essential learning is awakening— to not only deep depths of inner peace, to not only deep depths of seeing the cosmic cycle of creation and destruction as part of a whole, but at the very foundation or base, of feeling relaxed and rested in the unfathomable joy which manifests within all of creation! Be one with that energy; unite inwardly with that energy. Then you will find that there's nothing as worrisome as you had thought. There would be things, circumstances, events that come and go, but don't keep repeating your negative patterns mentally, psychologically. Be in a situation where you can wash away your guilt, your fears, your apprehensions through the act of enhancing joy within your heart and mind. It is a great catharsis, an inner cleansing process.

The greatest quality of a truly spiritual person is the ability to wash away that which has come upon him or her like mental dust: to *clean the mirror of your consciousness*. And the greatest 'cleaner' of that mirror of consciousness is the youthful energy of joy! It is like the joy of a newborn child: where he or she can look at things in a truly awakened, non-conditioned manner! In a manner which is beyond the distinction of 'right and wrong', sanctity or morality. Rather, as the Gita advises, be in your natural state. For then you find that you're able to enjoy the journey itself, in a manner which you had perhaps been missing. And when you enjoy the journey, the destination can never be too far away from you! It manifests successful living spontaneously.

CHAPTER-9

Beyond Happiness and Unhappiness Is Bliss!

Through the Gita, Krishna is taking Arjun on a journey which is beyond unhappiness and happiness. It is a journey towards bliss, towards ecstasy, towards mystical and spiritual happiness which transcends the duality of ordinary human emotions or states. This journey of consciousness itself takes you to a transcendence of feeling limited or anxious during tough times.

Usually, the human being is caught up between craving joy and escaping sorrow. And so doing, we are constantly oscillating between states of happiness and states of unhappiness. But the Bhagavad Gita is all about being in a situation where you attain a deep transcendental state from *both* these experiences. And come to such a harmony with the higher cosmic intelligence, that you become deeply blissful within yourself.

While this might be paradoxical—to understand that Krishna is taking Arjun on a journey which is *beyond* happiness and unhappiness—it is something to assimilate and perceive through the spiritual eye. It is not mundane.

Happiness and unhappiness can be sparked by so many factors. There are mundane states: every human being experiences them so many times a day. And keeps going between one and the other, depending on the particular feelings/emotions/ circumstances on the see-saw of life we are on. However, a great warrior is one who is neither looking for gratification, nor is he looking for creating sorrow for others. He's in a state where he's beyond both these situations. He is fighting within a state where his very being has dissolved into the greater. Where the very idea of death has been superseded by a transformative idea: of feeling one with the Cosmic Will that is running everything within this wondrous universe. It is a state of silence. It is a state where the impact of outer things cannot shake your inner being.

Our Inner Being

Arjun's *inner being* has been impacted in a very deep manner by *outer happenings*. But what Krishna is telling Arjun is that *no outer happening should be able to disturb the innate goodness within himself*. The innate eye of wisdom can perceive things in a much broader perspective. So the journey is one from narrowness of vision to a broadness of vision. It is setting onto a new path, a new way of looking at the world. One which understands that death cannot destroy us, but that we must encounter death no matter what, in a meditative state—in a state which does not worry us and is not a headache for us.

Hence, the Gita is a great experiment in the realm of the psycho-spiritual: it includes the questions of joy and sorrow, of happiness and unhappiness. But eventually, it says that these are not separate states! They are part of the same human reality. And to become super-conscious and transcend human limitations, we are to go beyond both extremes. If we do that, the fundamental purpose of mysticism is being served.

Eventually, in a spiritual sense, the Gita is about coming closer to the spirit, soul, or cosmic essence which resides within you and moving away from the sense that you are the body. The more identified with the mind-body complex you are, the less the possibilities of transcending happiness and unhappiness, and therefore, the less chances of going towards bliss. It is only when you identify yourself with that essence—that spirit, that soulful quality that you are essentially—is when this becomes possible. And Krishna's endeavour is to take Arjun on to that level of being where there is a certain disassociation from moods and feelings, from the psychological and the physical plane. And instead, there is an association with the soul— the microcosmic soul and the macrocosmic soul, the individual soul and the universal soul. In this manner, Krishna is taking Arjun beyond the state of misery.

In the spiritual context, even happiness can sometimes be a misery because it limits us. Unhappiness of course depletes us of energy. Hence, it is antithetical to finding a vastness of vision. Yet unhappiness is also sometimes the launching pad—a platform—for us to move on to the greater questions. Because it often makes us look at things in a much deeper way: as happens to Arjun, as happened to the Buddha. Only through that state do we become a witness of all that is going on.

Once you come to the state of witness-ship, it is all about being identified with your greater reality. Without this identification, everything is meaningless! You can see that Arjun has gone into a very deceptive state of mind at the beginning of the Gita. He has started dealing with falsehoods within himself, the deceptive state of mind which considers himself separate from the cosmic intelligence. Krishna is telling Arjun that he is part and parcel of the same cosmic intelligence. There is nothing that he, Arjun, can do which can disturb the order of the universe. He is just an instrument, he is just a part of that entire functioning. And he must play his part well! Only then will he come to a state of calm. And from that state of calm, move towards the state of bliss!

Beyond Anxiety

A deep anxiety had gotten an inner hold of Arjun's heart and mind. Hence, he behaves as if he does not even have the *physical* strength to pick up his bow and arrows. And it's literally described in the Bhagavad Gita, that he has put down his bow almost as if he is *completely* depleted of internal energy. And he is feeling very restless. So restless, in fact, that he's moving towards a state of *complete* weakness, of inner paralysis. Seeing this, Krishna does not advise Arjun how to be happy alone, how to be positive, or to practise so-called positive thinking! No, that is not the essence of the Gita! It is *not* about just thinking positively: it is about going *beyond positive and negative* (and hence, coming to a replenishment of one's internal spiritual energy).

Both the *positive* and the *negative* are aspects of the mundane and physical world, or the mental world of thoughts. But in the realm of the *spiritual* world, the positive and negative become one. These are sides of the same reality. It's like the Yin and Yang of the Taoists: they are opposites, yet form a different wholeness, oneness, and power, when they are together! They are not separate, they flow into one another. But the circle of the Yin and the Yang has a much greater meaning than the two aspects of it (the feminine and the masculine). It symbolizes that in life there are always two aspects of the rhythm: be it feminine and masculine, be it joy and sorrow, happiness and unhappiness, love and hatred, and so on. In the realm of the universal, these opposite things harmonize as part of the same greater reality.

So essentially, the takeaway from this is that in accordance with the state of *spiritual bliss* that Arjun has achieved, his mind-body complex will also function with a blissful and powerful energy. If at the level of the *spiritual* he is quiet, perceptive, sensitive, and is able to see the reality of things as Krishna describes them, then his functioning in the material world would not pose problems: he would be effortless in carrying out actions as needed. Hence, remember this always: solve your issue at the spiritual level, and you'd be able to effortlessly solve problems at the psychological and practical levels also.

Towards Mystical Understanding

The whole problem is that people first look for material accomplishment, and postpone their mystical or spiritual understanding. But it should be the other way around, because if spiritual and mystical light within your being comes, the whole burden of life becomes lighter! You're able to function in a much more effective manner. So at a very practical level too, the lessons of the spiritual are to be imbibed and put into action. Because they dynamize us in our day-to-day lives.

Several problems we have are based on a lack of spiritual insight. For example, let us look at the workplace. People often act in a manner which is immature, non-consistent: sometimes very angry, sometimes very friendly, and so on. In relationships, too, we are often not able to look at things with *an equal eye*. We all tend to become very agitated at some point. The state of agitation finds different expressions: often those of unhappiness with others. But the end result of it is that all this confuses us deep within, and does not allow our energies to integrate as one powerful energy. But through the mystical eye of looking at life—where you realize that with the negative comes the positive and vice versa, in a reciprocal flow—we can tide over things. Provided we are able to look at things with a spiritual vision, for this is when we truly start reaping the fruit of our efforts.

Right Effort

Sometimes our best efforts may end in failure. But this is more often than not because people are fragmented in their energies. One part of us is saying one thing, and the other part is saying another thing. One part of the mind may be saying that we be angry with a person we work with (or are in a relationship with), while the other part of us may be saying that we should be forgiving! So when you have such a split within yourself you're not able to come into the natural state of your intrinsic self. And eventually, coming to your natural, intrinsic self—your *svadharma* or *true nature* of being—is the essence of the Gita! The Gita implies that your intrinsic self is made up of bliss or ananda: this is the whole essence of India's thousands of years old wisdom. That at your very essence you are beyond both happiness and unhappiness, and you are simply comprised of bliss or ananda. That state is your ultimate state.

It is like the ancient Sanskrit mystic formula says, Sat-Chit-Ananda: from truth, to consciousness, to bliss! If you identify with that state of bliss, you start feeling that what you have been unable to resolve or have been fearful of, now simply becomes much easier to deal with. You start having the courage to go into things with boldness. You start feeling great freedom and fearlessness.

Hence, all these are very valuable lessons not only at the level of the warrior, but also at the level of a person in everyday life, no matter what position we are in. No matter what life situation we are in. The entire thing is to see the *largeness* of one's own being, and that can be seen only when we look at it as being comprised essentially of that blissful quality which permeates the vaster reality—a reality we may call God or Supreme Consciousness, or the Absolute Reality.

Expanse

Understand the *expanse* of yourself, understand the expanse of your life. And the best way to understand expansiveness is to look at things with the vision of bliss. When you do that, you will realize that everything is essentially made up of bliss: the plants germinating from the soil, the eagle flying high in the sky, the waterfall roaring down the mountain. Everything is a part of this essential cosmic bliss which is being played out in life. Without bliss, there cannot be this magnificent and wondrous universe. You can feel it at a very intuitive level, provided you are able to look with that vision.

Human consciousness is in a very precarious state in the world of today because it seems like religion has almost become irrelevant. Several concepts of religion have become redundant, and have been proven to be fake or false. But what is beautiful about a few teachings such as the Gita's, is that it is not about *absolute statements* or material facts to be corroborated by sacred texts. It is essentially about the states of consciousness which they talk about, which are the timeless questions.

Consciousness vs. Artifical Intelligence

Mankind today is faced with the situation where even artificial intelligence or AI is emerging as a real possibility and reality in our world. So the question arises: what is this thing called consciousness? What is the difference between human consciousness and what may emerge as highly advanced artificial consciousness? The gap between both seems to be becoming smaller. And from the spiritual perspective, eventually you can see that it is *the quality of bliss* which will differentiate between both. Human consciousness has the great potential to attain bliss, and it seems—at least in the foreseeable future—that *no matter* how complex a piece of machinery is, no matter how much its computing or perceptible power is, for it to come to a state of bliss seems rather unlikely, even if other aspects of human consciousness can be mimicked by its algorithms.

Hence, you can see that this quality of bliss is really the essential quality of consciousness. Identify with it more! Feel close to it. Feel its energy upon you. And then you will realize that it is our innermost reality! It will truly come alive in your life!

Open Your Mind

Sometimes we have to open our minds to a particular state of being in order for it to play itself to its full power in our everyday lives. Because when we open our minds to that state of being, it becomes easier to see its action within us and within the world. A small example: if you go to a sea beach with the attitude that it is very ugly, you'll see ugliness all around—be it the crowds, the garbage, and so on. But if you go to the beach with an open mind—no matter how crowded—and you look out into the horizon, you can find great beauty. Irrespective of how much tourist traffic or actual garbage may be on the beach, you can *still see* the vaster wonder: of sea meeting sky as an illusion on the horizon. And this in turn would actually empower you to make the beach cleaner and perhaps better, because you would like to do something to enhance the bliss experience for all!

So you can see that the positive impulse gives rise to positive action. You can see the importance of perceiving the bigger picture, the vastness of things. And seeing this vastness of things is what the state of bliss is! That is the state Arjun is moving towards in his journey, during the exposition of the Gita.

CHAPTER-10

Drop the Feelings of Remorse and Regret

The structure of the human mind is such that it keeps going back to things which it regrets, to something we may have done in the past. The past comes back to haunt us in various ways, consciously and subconsciously. This whole process creates a great mental storm and a mental conflict within us. It creates a mental habit of judging ourselves, of looking at things in retrospect: what we *could* have done or not done.

All this leads to a harrowing chaos in the mind, and the chaotic mind is exactly the mind you see within Arjun! His mindset on the battlefield is heading towards a feeling of great remorse. His mind is stuck in a rut during his tough situation.

Going beyond Regrets

Arjun is feeling a great deal of regret for fighting. He feels he is being partial to one side. He is feeling very remorseful for all the people he is going to kill. And what does Krishna do? Krishna tells him to completely drop this feeling of remorse, this feeling of regret and mental conflict! In any case there is no certainty in life, and in any case we are not the ultimate *doer of things:* things happen in the universe within which we are only participants, and not *creators* of. Therefore, get rid of worthless regrets! Don't let them create more trouble for you. Live in gratitude, live in simplicity. Live with wide-open eyes that do not get so embroiled into mental problems such that they poison your peace and equanimity.

Conflict in mind is sometimes worse than death: it's better for the warrior to fight in a state of equanimity rather than to live in a state of mental conflict and torture. That is the only spiritual thing which you can ultimately do: face death with absolute clarity of courage, without conflict! Only then can you experience the soul. Otherwise the soul cannot truly be encountered.

What Krishna is telling Arjun is not in order to impose any ideology upon him. It is in fact to make Arjun more conscious that it's absolutely imperative to do one thing: stop returning to the same root of regretful ideation and remorseful mental thought vibrations. Because in that process, Arjun is destroying all that is valuable in himself: not only as a warrior, but as a spiritual seeker also.

Being Masterful

Our whole spiritual quest in life is to be able to meet new realities in a manner where we are *masterful* within our own being, where we have faith in ourselves. And not be in a state where the past comes to haunt us, through the feeling of regret. Most people you'll find have a haunted look in their eyes. It's because there's always a question of what they *could have done*—in other words, avoided something which has negative repercussions today.

But that is not the point. The past cannot physically come back. The point is, no matter what we've done in the past, it is important to keep trust and faith in our hearts today. That is the only way we will be able to cope with the thorns and enjoy the flowers in life. And that is what peace of mind means. Peace does not mean a state of perfection; peace does not mean a state where sorrow does not exist. Peace means a state which is meditative, which has the power of transforming everything into sheer joy, which is capable of turning even hell into heaven! Hell and heaven are internal states within us, and in the transcendence of either extreme—of judging ourselves to be all good or all bad—we are able to come to that state.

Arjun is becoming mentally healthier and more whole in his understanding through the Gita, because he realizes that the only real sickness in life is the sickness of mental conflicts. That leads to a life full of shame because that is committing mental suicide within your very perception, within your very being. Now, Krishna is not afraid at all to be absolutely candid with Arjun, because Arjun is also his friend. Arjun is also his confidant. And Krishna is standing by him through all aspects of his life. But through the Gita, he wants Arjun to return home to that state of the conqueror who is absolutely full of energy, full of spirit, full of what the individual Arjun represents in his or her entirety. And what Arjun represents in his entirety is a certain nobleness of attitude. It is a certain nobility on the battlefield, an originality and strength which is always on the side of justice! Krishna admonishes Arjun for acting so worthlessly, simply because he is giving in to the feeling of remorse! Arjun is becoming quite useless by giving in to remorse. And that happens with us too: when we fall into a feeling of regret, when we fall into a feeling of guilt, we too become absolutely useless and paralysed and do not act as we are meant to act.

Clarity

Hence, no matter what we are— a leader, a musician, an inventor, a poet, a businessman—it is very important for us to have an inward feeling of such clarity that past sufferings do not come and haunt us. Don't suffer on account of yesterday! The true way of creative living is to move from one thing to the next with a feeling of non-regret in the heart, because that is the only way to nourish life. That is the only way to attest and affirm to the spirit of life itself. And in that lies true spirituality. In that lies the true fulfilment of potential. Anything can happen tomorrow, but it's all about being in a situation where within the very nature of yourself you are emptied of conflict. And conflict is within the mind.

Arjun's whole conflict is within the mind: *the conflict on the outer battlefield is the lesser conflict.* Over there, he can use his skill. But for the conflict within his mind, he's feeling very weak. And it is only through the heartfelt exchange between him and Krishna that he experiences things which are beyond words. He moves on to the more significant aspects of life, with great clarity.

Beyond Space and Time

The Gita is a catalyst or a trigger to know that phenomenon which is beyond space and time. In other words, it is a trigger to know that which is beyond the phenomenon of the mind's conflicts and regrets. The Gita takes Arjun on to a new understanding of reality. And this understanding of reality is really what going beyond the illusion of our material world truly means.

It is about unfolding our self-potential in the best way. The whole of the Gita is a resurrection of Arjun's inner power; a transformative resurrection. It is meant to encourage and stir his heart into creating *great action through great courage.* And that is what true dynamic living is all about. That is what true expansion of consciousness is all about. It is about feeling reborn every instant, with a great power, strength, and faith in what is to come.

Regret only leads to further fears. It nourishes and strengthens all that is negative in life. Avoid it; don't be fooled by it. It is an illusion. It is a psychological phenomenon, but on the mystical sphere of the eternal it is truly something which is to be discarded. Because it does not allow us to open up at our being's centre. It does not allow our spirit to fly upwards and ascend great heights.

A Flight of the Human Spirit

The whole process of the Gita is an ascension of the spirit, a flight of the spirit of Arjun. He is to be like an eagle flying in the sky, from where he can view the fullness of life and of creation itself, through the vision that Krishna helps him attain! Where he sees that life is not a mechanical thing to be lived in a mundane manner, but a luminous phenomenon within which we can be blissful partakers, no matter what! To understand the glory and depth of life itself is the message of the Gita. And it reminds us again and again that the truth of our being lies in absolutely letting go of all regrets, no matter whether our actions/efforts in the *past* have been successful at generating good or bad results.

No matter whether our past endeavours have been beneficial or not, it is the *now* which matters: *today* can be the moment of spiritual realization, today can be the moment of unifying with God or Godhead! Today can be the moment when you feel a beautiful new essence in your life. And all of your yesterdays can melt away, with their regrets, conflicts and so on! That is what true spiritual evolution means: that the presence of the divine is rich in you at every moment, such that there's nothing to fear! That is what Krishna represents. And through that feeling you come into a calm silence of your own being. You realize that real virtue lies in becoming clearer in your mind, because then you're able to absorb yourself in that which is foundational and *most important* in life. And not get lost in situations which are of guilt, of desire, of imagined problems and so on.

A Meditative Process

Through the whole meditative process of the Gita— this beautiful meditative interchange between Arjun and Krishna—all the frustration within Arjun seems to dissolve. When the frustration within himself dissolves, so do his regrets. And when regrets dissolve, he finds then the easy friendliness with Krishna restored once more. And through that, arise both great love and great dynamism in Arjun. Before that, he's as if on a rocky sea, and the waves are rocking the boat of his mind from side to side! There is no peace of mind for him. Essentially, Krishna makes him realize that when remorse is dropped and regret is dropped, peace comes as a real by-product. Peace comes as an abiding quality that is the very spiritual soul of life.

Even in his cosmic form revealed in the Gita, Krishna—with all his billions of terrible faces devouring all the warriors, and breathing in and out all the worlds in existence—is in essence a manifestation of that *peace eternal* which is the *progenitor of all things*! And through seeing this, Arjun very quickly realizes that his so-called regrets in life are very small indeed against the cosmic dimension.

The Cosmic or Universal Dimension

The cosmic or universal dimension of life is so vast, that it can immediately make us forget our regrets, our memories of painful moments in the past. And instead, *become aligned with the cosmic reality as it is in the present instant.* That cosmic reality is really always one which will make you expand your mind to such a degree that you can forget all that you *could have done, should have done*, and so on! All that *can be done* in the realm of consciousness is available: you simply have to be clear, and connected with self-belief. You have to be blissful. If you can do that, no challenge in the world can break you.

Real Richness

The real richness in life is that of consciousness. The real poverty is *lack* of higher consciousness. The real *strength* is the strength of consciousness. The real weakness is weakness in consciousness. This is what Krishna is again and again reminding Arjun. So, Arjun begins accepting this in entirety. This brings great clarity, peace, and silence within him! A great feeling of calmness enters his heart. He expresses this to the Lord, and is ready to be his genuine self, to show his real and original face as a warrior on the battlefield! Eventually, he comes to a resolution that he will *continue* to be that great warrior that he has always been. Moreover, he is imbued with a mystical and spiritual vision which he has now been privileged to have been given by the Lord.

It is almost that by the end of the Gita, Arjun has re-found a great treasure that he has within. And all regrets have fallen away from him, as if they were only imaginings! He had carried them for too long. He had been too attached to negative feelings. Now that he feels a bit of detachment from them, he also feels a great peacefulness, a great relaxation. He is absorbed and almost hypnotized by the mystic message of the Lord, and has become so serene that no problem seems like a problem anymore! The whole listening to the Gita itself has taken him to the point where he's become completely humble, but at the same time completely courageous! And it is only possible to be humble and courageous when you give up regrets, when you surrender your regrets. A person who doesn't do it can be neither humble nor courageous: there will always be a lingering fear, because things like regret and mental conflict always breed fear in their wake.

So the entire idea is to give up fear. It is to give up a situation where you are less than your highest self! Let it go. Find your uniqueness, and act in a manner as if there is nothing to regret. That is what true dynamism means. That allows you to live past tough times with a higher energy, courage, and wisdom.

CHAPTER- 11

Washing
the Consciousness Clean

The Gita is a washing of Arjun's consciousness. It is a deep cleansing process. Cleansing of what? Cleansing of wrong thoughts that are crowding Arjun's mind. And through this very cleansing process, Arjun's consciousness starts developing wings, starts taking flight towards higher realization! He starts perceiving the genuine answers to the struggles within this existence. Eventually, Arjun starts coming to a higher consciousness, and also to a state of devotion. He is able to soar past his worries and realize his highest potential as a warrior and an individual soul! That is how we must be during tough times.

The beautiful part about the Gita is that there is no question of sin or being a sinner. In fact, Krishna says that eventually no mortal being is *doing* anything at all: all is being *done* by a higher power. Yet our problem is that we *think* we are doing things, and in this very illusion of being the 'doer', we become lost and confused. Krishna tells Arjun to renounce these thoughts, and to once again be in that state where action comes out of a very clean space of pure being, from the deepest part of our being. That is the space the *real* warrior exists within.

Warriorhood

The warrior lives in a deep state of uncertainty: even the question of life and death are uncertain to him. He may not be alive the next instant! So he is to come into a state of surrender, if at all he wants to *evolve*. Because eventually the question of living or dying is not in his hands: he can only *do the best* he can. And that is what Krishna teaches Arjun, again and again.

Hence, with this cleansing of the consciousness, suddenly the flame of consciousness within the individual gets lit up! One's worldview starts changing. The same happenings go on, life goes on, but it's a way of looking at it which changes. And that is the most important thing: *it is not so much what happens, but how we perceive things happening which change and transform us from deep within.* Then only do we begin to see that the divine or greater power exists within us also, because we realize that within our own lives exists a consciousness of the higher. And that consciousness of the higher itself is a part of what we may call God or the Divine.

The Ultimate Warrior

The *ultimate* warrior reaches a state where he lets go of all material ambitions also. And once he or she does that, he grows in strength. He doesn't become weaker, because now he does not need to prove anything to the world. He attains a deep self-respect and a respect for life. And in so doing, becomes more individually integrated. And is able to bring himself to a situation where he feels something enlightened within him, something extraordinary existing within him! And that extraordinariness is simply the presence of the Divine, working through us. So everything he starts doing starts happening with more and more bliss; everything he starts attempting starts happening with less fear.

Being cleansed of fear is the most fundamental thing for a warrior before going into the battlefield.

To do our best requires us to be cleansed of persistent fears. Then only can we act dynamically, otherwise we would be paralyzed into inaction. So the act of cleansing implies that we come into such a state that we discover something more valuable than merely *the question of triumph or defeat.* It is not about being triumphant on the battlefield itself: *it is about being triumphant in the deep core of our own individuality.* And being integrated within is the greatest triumph. That is what true victory means. That is what true warriorhood means.

So, the Gita teaches this kind of warriorhood: it is not so much about conquering the world, it is not about conquering the enemy. Rather, *it is about conquering that fear deep within us,* which is part of our human conditioning. And when we conquer that fear, that conditioning, we move towards a feeling of being cleansed from within. And being thus inwardly cleansed we move towards joy, bliss, towards all those celebratory aspects of life which make it worth living! Else, life can be very dull.

The true warrior lives in a state of non-dullness, because he is cleansed of the feeling of inferiority or superiority. Krishna is convincing Arjun to be in a middle state of being, *where he does not feel superior to the enemy but at the same time he does not feel defeatist or inferior.* So Arjun's inner hopelessness is being destroyed, as well as his inner ego. Both are extremes. And both are part of falsehood. It requires a great deal of enthusiasm to function with ease, to function in a manner where we are dynamic no matter what we are doing. Now, Arjun is just an example. Essentially, the same lessons can be applied to any field of life; be it the world of business, the world of politics, the world of science and innovation, the world of the arts, the same principles apply! It is about being inwardly authoritative and finding beauty within ourselves.

Hence, the Gita is transcendent to particular situations. It gives us a completeness of view. The intention being that it makes us go back to the basic question of 'Who am I?'. It makes us go deeper into the very foundations of life and of our own existence. And so doing, we come to the most fundamental and individual part of ourselves. We come face to face with ourselves, minus the masks that we wear in our day-to-day functions.

The Most Essential

The Gita is really a very honest text which takes us to the most essential or genuine-most part of our being. All the darkness is expelled because the lamp of consciousness is lit by the teachings. And eventually the action of it is taking us towards a state of purity; towards a state where you feel things in a manner which is fresh and not burdensome . . . where you realize things in a manner that you can relate to the vaster and cosmic aspect of life itself. And so doing, you start vibrating with a renewed energy. You shake off the dreariness, the drowsiness of life and awaken to a fresh state.

Arjun has gone into a stupor, a drowsy state, a mentally stupefied state of anxiety. Krishna awakens him from this dark and drowsy state and shows him such light that Arjun's heart is filled with bliss. And he realizes that being dull, stupefied, burdened down by anxiety is not the way forward. The way forward for dynamic living is to do one's duty, but not at the cost of the destruction of one's inner integrity. Dynamic action has to come out of a space of deep faith within yourself; a state of devoted action. And that is the kind of state which Krishna is taking Arjun towards, where Arjun can distance himself from purely sentimental feelings about fighting his cousins and relatives. But at the same time he can be sensitive enough to see that it is all about a growth of consciousness that really causes us to be blessed in life. Otherwise life is very ordinary: it has no higher meaning. It is only this dimension of the transcendental that fills us with not only a gratitude and thankfulness for what we have, but also an opportunity to become servants of that cosmic power that is the very heartbeat and core of all things.

So it is about coming closer to the core of life itself, and so doing we become imbued with a meditative quality, become youthful, energetic, non-dull, and playful in our functioning. And thereby we come to a higher reality—one which allows us to look at the world with a fresh vision, and not with the tinted glasses of our conditioning. We are to remove these tinted glasses, and feel at one with reality. Reality as it is: in all its universal dimensions, as a pulsating and rhythmic harmony which has great love, beauty, and joy behind it all!

Krishna puts Arjun into that state where he's in touch with that bliss, that joy and ineffable love behind all of manifest existence. And so doing, Arjun starts coming to the mystical state: the spiritual state. And only in that state is there really a chance for us to live life in its broader cosmic dimensions, yet function dynamically within the world (in whatever we do)!

Who and Why

The whole emphasis of the Gita is in curing the problem about knowing 'who we are' and 'why we are here'. You see, in day-to-day life we don't even begin to ask 'who we are', but instead keep becoming greedy for outside goals. And that is the totally wrong direction! The most fundamental thing is to question and understand life itself, and through that very process comes about a purification of our motivations, a purification of our energies.

It is not necessary to find answers to everything! The search is important. And in that state of search itself, Arjun stumbles upon the voice of the Divine, which is close at hand. It is a possibility we all carry in life.

CHAPTER-12

Go with Nature

The Upanishads teach us that nothing can be done against nature. We cannot do anything which is not in harmony with the natural order of things and expect to succeed. The Vedanta says, 'Nature or *prakriti* is the reflection of the invisible Divine Consciousness, and is the determinant of all that moves or exists.'

Ultimately, nature is the determining factor of all things and of all results. What Krishna is teaching Arjun in the Gita is the vaster natural order of things: he is doing it in a mystical manner, but really the essence is that when it comes to nature—be it the cosmic order of things or the nature inherent within us as individuals—we must move according to its harmony. Then only do we attain fulfilment. Else we will constantly suffer and be in pain. Arjun is in great anguish and suffering, not relaxed within himself at all because he is trying to swim against the current of the cosmic river. Krishna is teaching him to swim with the current, to understand the cosmic element inherent within anything, and to work in consonance with that eternal energy which is both inside and outside of us. This energy constitutes the element of the divine. So doing, one's capacity for living to one's highest, even in tough times, is manifested spontaneously.

The Gita is all about the movement from the unnatural belief system of Arjun to the natural harmony and rhythm which Krishna is trying to inculcate within his heart and mind. With nature, all movement is ecstasy. Against nature, all movement is sorrow. So if you are to flow with the Infinite, you have to function in a manner where you are opening and absorbing more of essential nature and going with it. That way, the human being moves towards perfection. Otherwise we only move towards imperfection. And this is what is happening in Arjun's case: in one way he's stuck in the middle—he doesn't know whether to go left or to go right. He is completely stuck. Arjun is being helped by Krishna to come out of this rut. When he comes out of this rut, only then can he move and swim with the tide.

Man is so small and the universal dimension is infinitely large. We cannot expect to go against the universal order of things and succeed. Yet the universal order of things may be not as we perceive it to be. Our range of human perception is very limited. Even with the most advanced instruments, we can never quite measure that element which is behind all things, that element which is beyond material states and therefore cannot be measured by material means. The human being is stuck on the atomic and subatomic constituents of reality, but beyond it is the realm of the divine, the realm of enlightenment, the realm of the enlightened ones. That is the area which is hidden from us in life. And that is the area which really constitutes reality as it is because it contains the intrinsic seed of reality. So one is to go back to the seed state, go back to the soil and foundation of one's being and act therein with harmony. You see, it's like the seed: the seed must sprout in a manner which is consonant with the environment around it. If the seed and the soil do not match you cannot expect fruit and flower to come out of that plant. Each plant has a particular ecosystem to thrive within. For example, the cactus is the *rare* plant to thrive in the midst of a blazing desert.

This is also true in the material world of humans. For Arjun to thrive as a warrior, Krishna is encouraging him to do it through the present field of battle because in that lies Arjun's greatness. Our own individual capacities always find greater power when something deep within us is stirred and shaken so much that we go on to climb the mountain or the summit of achievement. Without this disruptive change, without this change of consciousness which Krishna brings about in Arjun, it is not possible for him to proceed with the great straightforwardness, courage and harmony of inner energy that is required within the heart of the warrior. Without this change in consciousness, Arjun cannot be efficient and effective on the field of battle.

Decisiveness

A warrior who is completely in a state of procrastination or non-decisiveness can never be truly effective, simply because he's incapable of dynamism. All dynamism comprises the ability to have complete and utter *quality of flow,* of powerful movement and decisiveness. Without decisiveness all things come to zero. This is true of the inner world as well as the outer world. You can see any leadership crisis or situation within our material world, our present-day world. All things which happen out of a state of calm decisiveness allow society to move forward, and all things that happen out of a confused state of leadership (through procrastinating) lead society to have a negative vibe. The very heartbeat of human consciousness depends on the dynamism which is available to it. And the ultimate dynamism is really not *doing* anything as such but *being in an inner tandem* with the rhythm of nature, the nature of our own consciousness.

When expanded, this principle tends to all things: it implies being in rhythm with the nature of the material world, and the nature of societal flow even. You can see that 'trends' in ideas and thoughts must be in tandem with the natural flow of things. Then only are they empowered, and find place in society through expressions in science, art, culture, business, and whatever else we can count as human pursuits.

But the whole thing is dependent upon moving towards a state of mental and spiritual liberation. That's the first step. Arjun needs to liberate his heart and mind. But how is he to liberate his heart and mind? Krishna again and again comes back to the same point: that *if Arjun acts according to his own nature, then he would automatically proceed towards liberation!* Else there is no liberation. Else there's only imprisonment of Arjun's spirit. To be liberated in spirit requires us to act according to our self-nature. Be yourself, as you are at your deepest levels! That is the ultimate Dharma. All other Dharma flows out of it. All duty-fulfilment must flow out of such a state. Then it is bound to create something good within the world. No good is going to come out by acting *against* it.

Cycles of Nature

Nature is cyclical. You can look at the seasons: spring is followed by summer, summer is followed by the rains, the rains are followed by autumn, autumn is followed by winter, and winter is again followed by spring. It moves in a cycle. And where there is a disruption of the cycle, there's bound to be suffering for people. Similarly, look at the revolution of the planets, and at the revolution of the galaxies. There is something *intrinsic* in nature, which we might call its essential spirit.

It is like the laws of physics, but at the same time it is not as narrowly defined as the physical or material composition of things. Because the 'x-factor' is there: the hidden element of consciousness, which is missing in ordinary studies of the material world. And it is not possible to *study it by material means* either. It is *an intuitive science*. It is a question of delving deep within our own consciousness, and from there coming to our own answers.

Essentially, what Krishna is doing is sending Arjun deep into his (Arjun's) own consciousness. He's doing it through his words, but essentially it is a going inwards, within-wards. And from that state,

Arjun begins to act as he sees fit, according to his own nature!

The Secret

The spiritual secret is this: Krishna can be likened to our deepest inner consciousness. He resides there, as the inner master. So in that manner the Gita can be taken as a metaphorical teaching: everybody has a Krishna within them. Act according to that voice of ultimate reality within you, that voice of ultimate consciousness within you. And then you will see that you do not spend life empty-handed. Then you will see that life becomes full of the immense vibe you derive from this inner voice. You start becoming energized by this inner voice. It is not a system of philosophy or thought ideas *from the outside*. Neither is it the exercise of a lazy person who does not want knowledge. Rather, it is the innermost search, and therefore the most intrinsically urgent search for a human being.

Becoming Free of Limitations

What Krishna is really guiding Arjun towards is a state of meditation: a state where Arjun's mind becomes completely free from limitations. Free from anger, from confusion, from desire, and so on. It leads to an emptying of Arjun's mind from such complexes. And from such clearing of confusion comes about a spontaneous response from Arjun. He responds to the call of the Divine, the song of the Divine, and starts feeling completely cool within his own being. He begins acting from that state of coolness. And eventually, the most fearsome warrior on the battlefield is one who can maintain composure even while being completely fierce! Who even while being completely warlike, can be composed. And this composure only comes when we act according to our own nature. If we are not acting according to our own nature, everything becomes a conflict. We cannot rise to greater realities, to greater heights, to greater mysteries.

Really, the idea is to be in a situation where we are peacefully witnessing the functioning of our own consciousness. That is the real state of meditation. In fact, this could be a definition of meditation:

peacefully witnessing the functioning of our inner consciousness, of our inner nature. Coming face to face with it. Coming face to face with that which Krishna represents: the deepest part of ourselves, which is connected to what you may call God or the Divine or the Absolute Reality. And functioning from that space in a manner which feels correct. Which feels like we can actually be dynamic in life. Which feels like it is the centre of your being. Which feels like now you are not going to 'miss the mark'. Which feels like you have come home! So this is the destination. The journey is through going within. And then you reach the destination, which is really the residing place of the voice of the Ultimate, the Higher. And when you reach this voice of the Ultimate, you can rejoice in its great feeling of peace. You can feel every cell within you imbued with energy. You can feel filled with a revitalized sense of being. And from this revitalized sense of being comes about a great feeling of wholeness, a great feeling that you are illumined within.

This is what Arjun feels eventually: like he's being illuminated within his own self. And so doing, he reaches a state of consciousness that has touched the deathless and timeless.

Science

Modern science or physics can only define things to a certain extent. Eventually, it is up to us to understand that science cannot possibly have *all* the answers because the realm of the material world is *too vast*. Yet, the intuitive sciences can have ultimate answers for life, and hence, they're worth going into. Consciousness is ours to explore as we wish. It is a shortcut to knowing the ultimate reality. That's why spiritualism will always be relevant. Because it exists in parallel with other developments of man, but at the same time it exists in its eternal dimensions. And it is accessible to all. It is not the property of one particular organization, or one particular institution. It is simply the changeless truth, it is simply that which can be expressed in infinite ways but cannot be touched and monopolized by any particular person. It is like one morning after another: always new, yet somehow echoing the mornings of yesterday. In a way, it repeats the past and the ancient, but it's still always brand new! In that way God is always new, because no sunrise can be the same as a previous one. It may have some similarity, but at the same time it has newness.

In the same way, our relationship with the divine element—which we may call Krishna—need not be the same as Arjun has. Each person's relationship with the divine consciousness can be unique. But the essential thing is that we are to be free of all fears, we are to be free to be ourselves. 'Being ourselves': that is the biggest fear people have, unconsciously—the fear of being and acting as themselves as nature created them in consciousness. Everybody wants to be somebody else, but being yourself is the only way to ultimately act. Because it not only brings you material results—by aligning all your energies to the greatest extent—but it will also bring you the grace of the mystical element in life. It will also bring you something that materialism cannot. It'll bring you the light of your own being! It'll bring you the light of spirituality. And that in the end is what ultimately fulfils us, not only as individuals but also in our actions as a responsible person of society.

People who can act according to the highest nature of themselves automatically become value adders to society. Because whatever they do is in consonance with a greater good. They might not be doing it for that purpose, but their actions spontaneously have a quality of serving a larger purpose.

And this is what Krishna is trying to tell Arjun: that when Arjun acts according to his self-nature, and when he acts dynamically, he will also become a great example for society. Else he will only bring dishonour, he will only bring suffering upon others. So, first, act according to your nature! And the results for society too will follow automatically. Become a positive contributor instead of a negative one.

Leadership

It's become very important in the world of today for leaders to be great examples. It has always been so, but now leadership has reached a position where at the same time one can reach millions of people through electronic means and technology. So every subtle vibe of a leader becomes intrinsically important. Hence, the question of consciousness and the question of the Gita itself has become more and more important. It is a text for the future, not only for the present or the past. Because it has a template which is very practical.

It gives us the greatest lessons on not only how to live as human beings but as leaders and members of a broader community—as citizens of a common Earth, a common solar system, a common galaxy and cosmos, and so on. That is the timelessness of the Gita.

No matter whether the human species will explore the faraway stars in the future or even settle on other planets, the Gita will *still* have relevance. Because it is concerned with those ultimate questions which will always be of relevance to anybody with a consciousness. It takes away the question of 'human' or 'non-human'. It goes into *the question of consciousness itself.* And essentially the golden rule is to act according to your *deepest* consciousness because according to Krishna, that is also your *highest* consciousness. At the heart of understanding consciousness is this principle or 'key': the deeper you go into it, you'll find that it has very high and noble impulses. Even if a person seems wicked in ordinary life, at his highest state of consciousness even he is capable of being enlightened! Of being a Rishi or a Buddha! Of achieving *moksha* or nirvana. In fact, this is exactly what the Rishis of the Upanishads and Vedas said. This is what Gautama

Buddha also says, that if a person acts according to his truest consciousness, automatically, she or he becomes a force for good. Nothing he can do will be wrong. All that he does will be right. So this is the Golden Rule, a truth that has stood the test of time for thousands of years.

Whether it was Krishna's time or Buddha's time, the greatest avatars, the greatest teachers have taught this fundamental Golden Rule. It is not a rule as in an ordinary physical law for a particular space-time and which is frozen in its idea implications. But it is rather an intuitive concept which is applicable timelessly. So you've had people like Zarathustra, Mahavira, Guru Nanak, Kabir, Jesus of Nazareth, Ramana Maharishi, all of these great mystics throughout the ages and throughout the world have echoed this Golden Rule in one form or the other. It is universal. It is a master key to living one's best in tough times.

CHAPTER-13

From Despair to Dynamism

What Krishna is telling Arjun in the Gita is to fight without ego. Even as an archer, Arjun will find it easier if he leaves the ego, because only in that state we come closest to perfection. Otherwise, everything is frustrating, everything causes anxiety and despair about results, especially during tough times.

The art of the Gita is in teaching us to be able to function as if we are just an instrument. So, Arjun is not the archer: he's the bow of the Lord. The Lord shoots the arrows through him. Now, what happens in that dynamic state of consciousness is that suddenly Arjun starts finding himself to be a part of a cosmic whole and not chaos.

So far, Arjun has been in an inwardly chaotic state, till he listens to the Gita. But the real thing is that this chaotic state has been brought about by the various thoughts floating in his mind: all sorts of possibilities floating in his mind. And he is not really attentive to the essential thing! In the end it is only the quality of attention that we bring to a thing, which determines the outcome of whatever our action is.

Hence, in order to find the courage, in order to feel like he is unshakable in strength, Arjun has to get rid of the inner doubting which he has constantly. But the primary condition to do that is to not be led astray by thoughts. Rather, one is to be in such a state of automatically functioning in the manner of being an instrument of God Himself.

So far on his journey in the epic of the Mahabharat, Arjun had never utilized himself as an instrument of a higher power. He had been functioning as Prince Arjun the Warrior: deaf to the voice of that Consciousness which is greater than ourselves. And only in that Consciousness is true energy, strength, and vitality found! If we connect with that state, we will become filled not only with bliss but with great inner strength: such strength that cannot be moved or shaken by unconscious doubts, anxieties, and fears!

So the whole struggle of Arjun is towards coming to the correct moment; in glimpsing the glory of the greater consciousness working through himself. His mind is otherwise a great crowd of ideas, but to come out of this crowd of ideas is the whole thing! Arjun is too concerned about his own self: he is not seeing that light of wisdom can come from beyond his individual mind. And imbue not only his mind but his actions within the battlefield as well. And that light comes as the light of the Gita! Through it, he feels imbued with such an energy and strength that he throws away the crutches of anxiety and thought! Essentially, we always use our thoughts as a crutch to justify things; but Krishna takes away those crutches from Arjun, and leaves him in a state where he realizes that he is completely bare! And in spite of his anxieties, he can act with great joy and happiness in the moment that comes before him.

True Strength

Suddenly and unexpectedly, Arjun feels imbued with great strength. He feels that he need not be an inwardly disturbed or over-aggressive warrior on the battlefield, but can be extremely powerful without being violent in approach. It is the skill which comes into play, and skill is always hampered by our emotions of violence, our emotions of aggression or jealousy, or our feelings of sadness. Take away those, and you find yourself working with pure bliss and ecstasy. And that is not something any amount of skill can give you! That is what it means to be a warrior in the spiritual sense: where whatever process you are undertaking is a flow, is a constant streaming of energy through you. And you can function without hesitation! You can move dynamically forward without being stopped by hesitation, because now you are totally in your action! You have attained a state of non-intellectual action, which is suffused with the great wonder and power of courage which dawns on you. This is true passion: not the passion which thoughts and feelings convey to us, but a passion which makes us realize that there is a higher calling.

Hence, it is not about knowledge and gaining knowledge, but rather about *not making distinctions between things:* being choiceless in whatever situation you are faced with! Then a great churning of energy happens within you, and the 'wheels' of your strength start turning faster and more dynamically. It's very symbolic: the whole idea of the 'chariot'. The chariot of Arjun has come to a standstill, the wheels have stopped moving, but after getting the light of wisdom from his divine charioteer, the *Sarathi or divine guide* Krishna, the wheels of Arjun's chariot can move forward in battle with great dynamism! The idea is this: the divine message is one that makes us move forward the 'chariot' of our own action, in an extraordinary way! By taking us out of our so-called logic and self-justifications.

So in this manner, like Arjun, we can begin feeling that we are not relying *only on ourselves,* but also attain maturity enough to understand that it is the entire mechanism of the cosmos within which we are functioning! And that we are only a part of it, and in that part which we have been given, we must display a great deal of passionate action! Passionate action does not arise by merely philosophizing, by getting into the groove of knowledge. Come out of the groove! Come out of the rut, and start relying on your own *higher consciousness*. In this reliance of higher consciousness is the secret of dynamic living: no matter if you are a leader, no matter if you are part of a team, no matter if you are aiming for what others feel is impossible!

Activate Your Consciousness

Hence, the whole and ultimate idea is to activate the wheels of your own consciousness to a degree where you can very spontaneously and momentously bring the fullness of your own energy into the task which is faced by you. The endeavour is to do away with the discomfort which you have been feeling within yourself; to remove those barriers which you have been feeling within, and move towards not only a state of spiritual health but, mentally, towards a state of equilibrium also. All of which naturally has an effect on whatever material and physical action you need to carry out. The body, and the skill sets we have, are only servants to what the mind suggests to us! And the mind is a servant to that wondrous thing called higher consciousness! So essentially, it boils down to that. And when it comes to the work we do, do it with more love and patience. But also with such a great deal of strength, which perhaps you have never realized you have within!

In moments of despair or weakness, remember this: the Divine rekindles your consciousness. That is exactly what Krishna does: he rekindles the higher consciousness of Arjun. And so doing, takes him from despair to dynamism.

CHAPTER-14

Being A Channel for Higher Truth

One of the most fundamental aspects of Hinduism (Sanatan Dharma) is the rishis'/ sages' teaching that ultimate knowledge is always revealed to one *from beyond the individual mind*. In other words, it is only when the ego of the individual mind disappears does higher knowledge and deeper truth descend unto the 'seer' or sage. The person of truth in life, as per Hinduism, is merely a listener (*shraavak*) and a channel (*maadhyam*) for higher truth. In the Mahabharat, Krishna represents the Beyond, the Vast, whose voice echoes as the Bhagavad Gita. He is making Arjun a receptacle or channel of truth. And so doing, Arjun is able to rise above the challenges during the tough time he is facing, and emerge victorious.

Hinduism asserts that the highest spiritual truth (*sat*) is inherent in the fabric of the universe, within its every particle. And the mind can only be a channel or medium within which this truth can reverberate. All so-called truths which are created by the mind and by limited thoughts are actually only half-truths, and are often falsehoods. The sages say that most of us spend our lives believing these very falsehoods. The mind imagines for itself its own reality. And this concept is increasingly being echoed in science too: all that we knew yesterday to be absolute scientific truth is washed away by today's discoveries (for example, Newton's mechanistic worldview of the cosmos was shattered by Einstein, and Einstein's theories themselves are up for challenge in an age of advanced quantum physics).

So, this is the essential problem of man: we keep building our own stories from within our own minds. We become creatures of psychology instead of being identified with spirituality, which we essentially should be. The entire movement towards fulfilment in life has to be one where you're able to access greater truth, that which is beyond the individual mind. Do not go by your own imaginings, what your mind suggests to you, because that truth is always limited. It keeps the perception of yourself and the perception of your potential (the perception of what you can do and not do) always limited by its own boundaries. The mind creates its own boundaries, and that is its biggest weakness. Sometimes it is a strength because it is a defence mechanism (fear also is a defence mechanism as it often saves us from catastrophe). But eventually, to be really content in life and to move towards true wellness of mind, body, and spirit, we are to move towards that fearless state and original state which is beyond the level of thought itself.

The human being, from the ancient Hindu point of view, is much more than a creature of thought: we *think* we are who we are, but that is not the ultimate truth of ourselves. The illusion of man is getting identified with his name, his position, and so on. But eventually your true potential is always rooted in the very source of yourself, and not what your parents or society have told you. The very deepest impulses of your being lie rooted in the deeper aspects of existence. And if you can tap that, then life spontaneously becomes transformed. This is the experience of the seers, the rishis or the sages. In fact, this is what the Upanishads are all about.

Hence, a deeper exploration into the very roots of yourself is key. And from there whatever action arises, starts becoming dynamized. Whatever friendships you have, whatever relationships you have, whatever your view of the world, whatever your insights, whatever your attitude within the world, all start becoming dynamized too! Because now all arises from the deeper space within yourself. And when you act out of the deeper space, you feel incredibly linked to the very throb of universal energy! And being so linked to universal energy, you don't feel dull. You feel expanded, more confident: filled with an inner light! And this light shows and portrays itself in all that you do. You are able to go beyond the doubt-creating mechanism of the mind.

Going beyond Constant Doubt

The mind is a perfect doubt-creating mechanism: it always keeps us in a state of restlessness. And the sages say that it often deceives us: this very restlessness, this very anxiety and worry deceives us into believing many falsehoods about ourselves. We cling to the smaller portions of ourselves. And by clinging to the thoughts and anxieties about ourselves, many mental illnesses start manifesting. For example, some people get caught up in the syndrome of hypochondria: imagined illnesses. Some people get caught up in a sense of financial insecurity about the future. Some people get caught up about how best to resolve troublesome relationships (they are unable to deal with relationships as their human and social skills feel inadequate to themselves). According to the ancient view of the Hindu mystic philosophers, this happens because we are led by the mind, and hence by the ego. The fullness of our heart ('heartfulness') can only be realized through feeling and having faith deep within.

So, it is not our mind which is the creator of our destiny, but our sense of feeling that we are connected to divinity—whether we know it or not. Being so connected, you feel light. You feel as if the burden of mental ego and thought processes has been taken away from yourself. And so, by feeling light, you are able to function with great naturalness and dynamism. Eventually, the most efficient way for a human being to function is to be in a naturally dynamic state, in a fluid state of energy where mental energies, physical energies, emotional energies, and spiritual energies are all aligned into doing what has to be done. This creates a certain sweetness of living, this creates a certain bliss in whatever you do. Then your work does not feel like it is dull. You begin going beyond the logic of your limited mind and enter into a playful state which the mystics always talked about. That playful state of man is really the basis of all happy energy. That playful state is the basis of all meditative energy, of concentrated energy. Of energy which has the power to take you beyond your sense of having limited potential, into an unlimited space where all worries and anxieties become meaningless. You start becoming receptive to a greater power, and being receptive to a greater power actually empowers in present-instant living. So essentially, it is all about being able to empower yourself through the action of going beyond the mind, of being a medium or channel of the higher. Which is what Arjun realizes through the episode of the Gita.

Wholeness or 'Purnata'

A central crux of Hinduism (Sanatan Dharma) is that we are to feel very much a part of the wholeness (*purnata*) of the universe. This very feeling of being integrated with the wholeness of the cosmos is the seed of well-being and harmony in life. It relaxes us at a very deep level. And this is what the sages used to teach. It is what echoes through the Upanishads and the Gita. The feeling of wholeness is a key principle for living in a fulfilled manner especially during tough times.

Ultimately, success and spiritual liberation both lie in coming to a sense of wholeness, and not feeling like you are incomplete or alone. Because if you feel incomplete or alone, anxiety arises. Then it becomes all about individual accomplishment, and your eyes are focused only on a very narrow periphery of self. The sages say that being too narrowly focused takes us away from our broader reality. And only in a sense of our broader reality do we feel a great joy, a great energy of wellness, a feeling of potential realization within ourselves. And that is the very root—the very foundation—of all great things that are to be done in life! Else, we are only groping in the dark, because we are only running after a very small definition of success.

Real success occurs when your energies are going in one flow towards finding oneness and wholeness with the universe, through the process of finding a sense of total identity and 'being' with all that exists. This is the secret of getting rid of all our mental repressions too.

From the Gita's point of view, our anxieties have a root in our sense of 'separateness' from the wholeness of the universe. In this light, the teachings of Vedanta and of the Gita are far more advanced than any psychology or any therapeutic means of mental health, because they teach that it is all about the micro-consciousness coming into an attunement with the macro-consciousness of the universe. In this way Hinduism is not only humanistic, but is also profoundly rooted in the science of mind: it goes to the very depths of what it means to consciously get rid of fear. Because if you feel a oneness even with the unknown, then the whole question of fear disappears! You see, the most basic fear in man is the fear of the unknown. And the unknown is nothing but the vastness of existence itself. So Hinduism says, and the Rishis say, that if you embrace this vastness within your mind and heart, then what happens is you spontaneously become calm! All your fears evaporate, as if they are just mist, just illusions.

Hence, the whole secret to successful living is to bring about—not in an enforced manner—a sense of oneness with all things. And to find great beauty in the vast spaces of existence. You see, the greatest power that man has are intellect and the power of wonder. Creation itself is marvellous, but human beings lose the eye of seeing things in this marvellous fashion. The viewpoint of the sages is that the whole climax of life has to happen in an integration and oneness with this very vast and simply wondrous creation/universal energy that we are part of. Else all our effort in life does not bring us a fullness of results. We remain only partially successful. Complete success and complete grace in life implies that you go beyond the approach of looking at things in a piecemeal manner, and instead look at things in a manner of oneness. A manner of wholeness. Which is what Arjun is made to see!

The fragmented mind cannot find true fulfilment. The integrated mind is one which finds true fulfilment and true contentment. And it is also the mind which is not dull, which is full of energy because it feels joined to a greater energy. And that greater energy transforms you from within!

Ultimately, it is all about the level of consciousness that we function from that determines how truly fulfilling life is to be. If you function in an inwardly luminous manner, all things become luminous and bright. Your very being becomes bright, your very demeanour towards others, your very relationships and the very vibe that you create in the world assumes a stance of positive energy. And through that positivity of energy comes about the miracle of real success.

A fragmentary approach will not do! Fragmentation leads to lack of clarity. Clarity only comes about by seeing the greater picture. It is like the eye of the eagle: the eagle flying high above can see with a fullness of vision. So even while it is detached from what its watching, it's vision is much clearer. It's able to identify what it needs to do. It's able to identify the battles it needs to fight. Yet at the same time it feels a great freedom of flying in the sky! And that is what human life should be about: to fly in the sky of consciousness as a free person, because that is eventually what spiritual freedom means. To feel freedom. And the best way to do that is to feel conjoined and unified with the vastness of existence itself. In that way, your energies do not dissipate into anxiety, but rather integrate into a great oneness of being which fulfils you at every level.

Human life is a search for a situation where you are completely fulfilled. Where you are not dull. Where you're not bored. Where new things come to your vision, where you feel renewed every instant: inventive and creative in your own way, according to your own skills. Because that creates a happiness of energy within you. And the best way to do so, say the sages, is to feel like this entire creation is yours! That it belongs to you, and that you belong to it, completely! In that manner comes about a union of heart and mind. And most of all comes about a great delight in being itself! It is the enjoyment of your inner being, which cannot be neglected any longer: it should be the focal part of human efforts. If that is right, all goes right!

Life Positivity and Spiritual Freedom

The basis of being life-positive is the ability to feel spiritual freedom, freedom within yourself, deeply. It is the key to dealing with tough times.

This is the very basic crux of the whole spiritual search: a movement towards inward freedom. But most of the time religion does just the opposite: it imprisons people within a set of belief systems deep within themselves, whereas the truly mystical path is one of attaining true freedom in heart, mind, and soul. This liberates and releases life positivity within you. And imbued with life positivity, you begin to achieve things which you had perhaps not even thought possible!

So this is the fundamental crux of what the Gita itself teaches. Krishna is trying to free Arjun from the grip of mental restrictions, by bringing his mind into a deep relaxation and a letting go of his conditioned concepts. Krishna destroys Arjun's prison of thoughts, and breaking free of the prison of thoughts, Arjun steps out as a calm, collected, and most powerful warrior.

The essence of warrior-hood is to attain an inner quietness, calmness. But that comes only by opening the locks of the soul, the locks of the heart and mind. Then a great power starts arising within you and begins affecting your actions in a positive manner. You see, the whole problem is that throughout our lives we have been taught to repress or to feel guilty. To not give true expression to who we are. But Krishna says very boldly in the Gita that the only real spiritual action is that which is born out of non-repression. That which is born out of freedom! Hence, be free in your action. Then you will find that you have great power! Be exposed, do not be clammed in within yourself (as Arjun is in the beginning of the Gita). That is what being an individual truly means. Where you respect the sense of freedom within yourself; and respecting the sense of freedom within yourself, you feel liberated in a manner which cannot be compared.

The Buddha used to say that Buddhahood is within all. And that is what the Gita is saying, in a slightly different manner. That you are full of the light of enlightenment: you just have to know it, believe it, trust in it! And then a consciousness arises, where you become a force of great positivity in the world. Otherwise your mind is constantly moving in a destructive loop. And moving in a destructive loop leads to psychological illness. Arjun has gone into a deep psychosis of being. He is committing suicide within himself by not acting as he is meant to act! Krishna tells him to instead commit a spiritual suicide where he lets his old self shed like the skin of a snake and emerges new! It is a process of catharsis. It is a process of chrysalis, like the butterfly emerging out of the caterpillar.

History has produced great warriors, but most of them have been forces of destruction. You can look at Genghis Khan, Napoleon. You can look at so many kings, conquerors, and generals throughout history. But there are those few, rare warriors who work with a sense of spiritual freedom within themselves. And that is what real warrior-hood means. This was what the samurai codes also represented. The samurai warrior, before going into battle, wrote a death poem: it was meant to express his innermost being, it was meant to free all his latent potentialities. And then when he went into battle he went as a free person. Not as a repressed person. All his energy became available to be put to the cause of the war! To the cause of justice, the cause of the battle that he was fighting. And this is the very essence of what it means to be a warrior.

Krishna very boldly tells Arjun that he cannot kill his enemies' souls, he cannot kill his enemies' spirits. Therefore, he should not grieve! Krishna tells Arjun that he is just releasing them from their human bodies. And that is what the true warrior is doing: he's not harming his enemies at a spiritual level. It is just like a game being played out by the divine. The Mahabharat is not an unfair battle where Arjun is told to go and kill innocent people. He is facing an army, so it cannot be called an aggressive action against innocents. It is simply a duty-led responsibility which Arjun has on his shoulders. And remember, Arjun represents what every leader is meant to be! Every leader is supposed to lead his team into battle by setting an example himself. It's about how he himself leads, fights, charges, and displays internal calmness and equanimity, which sets the whole example for his team.

So if you look at the Gita in the context of leadership, it becomes very important to absorb its lessons about warrior-hood. It is eventually a case where you are not really fighting for a religious ideal. In fact, religious warfare throughout the ages has been some of the most destructive and pernicious warfare. Because it is based on some vague concept of fighting for a particular 'belief'. But here, it is fighting out of freedom from all beliefs! It is fighting from a state where the warrior Arjun is to not continuously think of any particular scripture while he's fighting. It is a state of true spiritual freedom which is the touchstone and the test of what he is doing. Krishna is telling him not to over-analyze the amount of destruction that he is going to do on the battlefield. Because the enemy has no such qualms! The enemy is simply there to win by any means, and therefore, it is beholden upon Arjun to do as the circumstances dictate. The whole political structure of civilization is at stake, the whole social standing is at stake. And in a big way, it is resting upon Arjun's shoulders, because if he loses hope his entire army will lose hope. And thereby, they will lose the battle. This will lead to a very negative leadership, because the other side has some very negative leaders like Duryodhan who are simply hankering for the crown. They will not be good for the people.

Therefore, what Krishna is advising Arjun to do is free himself from all the fetters and chains that he has placed upon himself. These mental chains are to be removed by ourselves: that is the beauty of spirituality. We can shed our own limitations; this is the dignity of man. So Krishna imbues great dignity upon the individual, upon man, because man himself (through his will) has the ability to break free of his spiritual conditionings, of his knowledge conditionings, of his social and political conditionings. And emerge as a spiritual being who is ready to fight or to lead as the situation demands! But never in a manner which is pernicious or evil; always in a higher state of consciousness. And whatever comes out of a higher state of consciousness always leads to happiness and freedom for other people too. It not only frees us within our own selves, but leads to good within society. So it is incumbent for us to act in an intelligent way and not run away from the fight, whatever it may be.

Arjun feels like there are heavy chains of responsibility upon his shoulders. That is true: he does have great responsibilities. But at the level of the spiritual, it is very important for him to attain an inner harmony and organic sense of freedom within himself (if at all he is to express his warrior skills to their fullest extent). Therefore, what he is taught by the Lord is that no matter what happens, he's simply to function in an effortless manner, where his skill is set free and released to do as it needs to do. Then automatically and spontaneously, the best part of Arjun will come into action. And when the best part of Arjun comes into action there is nothing to fear about whether the results will be one of victory or defeat.

It is simply a question of expending our energy in the best possible manner which leads to our evolution. In order to evolve, it is very important for the individual to feel free in the mind. Because the mind can create limitations, and the moment limitations are there they become like a wall which we cannot cross. Free the mind! This is essentially Krishna's message. And through the Gita, Arjun's mental walls and mental blocks start melting like ice. You see, the Gita has a great cooling power on the mind, but it also has a property of heat: it has the ability to melt those frozen aspects of ourselves which are not flowing. Like an iceberg, they can become an obstacle on the movement of the ship of life. But we have the ability to melt those icebergs with the fire of consciousness. And the fire of consciousness is the Gita in its true essence!

The whole essential teaching of the Gita is not one of character, is not one of moral codes or normal 'morality'. It is one of something much larger. What is at stake is consciousness itself. What is at stake is being life-positive. What is at stake is being free to the extent that one flows with great dynamism into whatever one is doing, with wide-open eyes. And so doing, one moves towards what the Buddhas have called the 'field' (*kshetra*) of the Buddhas. Here at Kurukshetra it is the field of battle, but even the battlefield becomes transformed into a field of enlightenment for Arjun! So it is up to us: every field that we are in can be turned into a field of enlightenment. It just requires us to see with the right vision. It just requires us to feel refreshed by the thought that we can be completely free, and to free the mind at any given instant. There is nothing to bind us but ourselves! We can melt the walls that we have placed around ourselves in the form of ideas, and so doing the ray of cosmic and divine light enters us and makes us even more dynamic in whatever we are doing.

CHAPTER-17

From Questions to Answers

When you ask the important questions then does the Divine answer you. This is a secret of the Gita. Arjun keeps asking questions of the Lord, and Krishna very patiently replies to his questions. Yet the moment one particular question is answered, Arjun has another and then another, and so on. And the Lord continues to answer. But the essence of it all is that Arjun is a questioner, he is a seeker. So that much will and courage we have to find within ourselves: ask the penetrating and important questions. Then the answers will come from the divine or higher consciousness, here signified by Krishna. All religions of the world in fact echo this truth: Ask! Don't hesitate. The greater power is at hand within you to help you. You are never distant from the greater power of the universe: realizing this, you feel filled with great courage and higher consciousness during tough times.

But the whole point is to look at the essential things, the spiritual basis of who we are and what our function in life is, as Arjun does. When you look at the essential things, then only do the questions well up within you. That is spiritual thirst, that is the beginning of the journey of being enlightened. Ask, search, and then you will find. Great mystics like Kabir and Jesus say a similar thing. If you don't search yourself, and if you don't ask those penetrating questions, how can you expect your problems to be resolved? Problems *do* resolve, provided we begin walking the journey with an expression of the right questions. Through this process, we develop a very intimate relationship with the divine element. You see, what Krishna represents is that the divine is always available to us, to help us when we are low. Yet if we do not come into an intimate relationship with the divine by truly questioning life, by truly going deeply into those questions which are important, then what is the whole point? Then we just live for a certain number of years, gain a little knowledge, gain some skills, earn some money, and die. And the mystery remains unknown to us.

Creation is a great mystery, and it is only through probing into the mystery that you can expect something to come out of your life. All significant endeavours in human history have happened through asking the right questions till we come upon workable answers. And the workable answer will come at some point. Look at Thomas Alva Edison. He discarded thousands of ideas that did not work before he finally stumbled upon the correct way of creating the electric bulb. Similarly, though in a quite different context, Albert Einstein began by questioning what can be and what will be the possibilities within the cosmos, through his thought experiments. As a result of these thought experiments he came to some answers which transformed the human understanding of science.

In the realm of the spiritual sphere also, the

highest texts are always about questions and answers: be it between the boy sage Ashtavakra and King Janak in the Ashtavakra Gita, between Prince Ram and Rishi Vasishtha in the Yoga Vasishtha, be it between Gautama Buddha and his charioteer Channa when he first went out of the palace. His questions arose: about suffering, about death, about sorrow, and so on.

So, the thirst to find the answer *brings* the answer to you. Therefore, it is very important to be inquisitive. As a human virtue there is no substitute for this search, this thirst, this inquisitiveness. The Wright brothers asked themselves how they can make flight happen, and eventually they made it happen. So be it science or technology, be it spirituality or mysticism, philosophy or the arts, everything can be traced back to a process of having a real willingness to go deep into that which we may see as a problem. Because out of that will emerge the answer to the problem. And solving a problem is true creation of value.

Hence, to be a person of value requires us to ask, like Arjun! Yes, we may not literally have a Krishna in close physical proximity to us. But in the realm of consciousness we can go deep and therein approach the divine element of life (or what we can call the super conscious part of ourselves) to answer us. The deeper we go into consciousness, the greater the answers come. This is the promise of all the great mystics throughout the world, through the ages. And this is essentially what yoga is, what the whole search for nirvana or enlightenment is—a synthesis between questions and answers.

To be an adventurer, risk-taker, true leader, or innovator of any kind requires us to step out into the unknown. Out of our comfort zones! That is what creates something new in the world. And giving something new to the world is the pinnacle of human achievement. Else our lives by themselves have little meaning. So the essential principle is that growth always happens because of an internal struggle within ourselves. When we don't find the answers, when we stumble and fall, then sometimes the most profound answers come to us.

It is like the seed germinating: it has to break out of the hard shell! And that is what the Gita is. Arjun is breaking out of his shell of enclosed ideas and has begun questioning. And when he does that, he finds that in a very short span of time he moves towards an understanding of the cosmic element of life. This eventually brings him not only bliss but takes him to the correct path for his life. It aligns his mind in the right direction. So this is a mystical thing to understand: we can call it 'right questioning'. We can call it attaining harmony through an initial chaos. Questions can be chaotic, but eventually they lead to harmony.

It's like tuning a musical instrument: while tuning it, it sounds like it is chaotic and just noisy. But once it is tuned, it can create a massive vibration of energy, a great beauty. And that is the gift of 'harmony': being aligned to the universe's energy. Be it through music, be it through our work. For Arjun, this alignation with the universe happens through his role as a warrior. It's all a question of uncovering those hidden treasures within us which are part of our essential makeup.

It's okay to have a burdened mind, it's okay to have a mind which is confused. Arjun is confused! Almost every human being is confused at some point in their life. Only the know-it-alls are never confused, because they seem to have the answers to everything! Now, Buddhas are not confused, they are clear; but most intelligent people always have some degree of confusion, because there's so much unknown to them. They're always struggling with problems; but the thing is to explicitly tap into the power of our unconscious minds. To go deep within, in a meditative process. And out of that will come those answers which will calm us, relax us, align us with the universe. For example, in a meditative state you can go into the feeling *that you are the sea itself and not the waves of the sea:* you can start becoming more identified with the *deeper aspects* of yourself. You can start feeling that you are one with that procreating consciousness behind the universe. And so doing, you realize that you are part of the divine itself. And being part of the divine itself, no problem seems like a problem anymore. You begin functioning with grace, with ease, with a tensionless dynamism. And that is eventually what happens to Arjun also on the field of battle: he starts functioning in a manner which is extremely full of awareness and strength.

Attainment of real awareness and strength cannot be through a process which is forced on you from the outside, or through an external discipline. It has to happen through your inner consciousness, through the chemistry of your own bio-spiritual being. It needs to be spontaneous. For spontaneity is in the realm of intuitive knowledge. Where there is intuitive knowledge, there is spontaneous growth. Intuitive knowledge is the mystic quest, it is in intuiting those questions which are essential to you. And not shirking them out of fear. Face your fears! And then do you attain courage and open up to life.

Arjun's whole quest before Krishna is in opening up of that which is plaguing him. He is opening up with his problems. And once he begins opening up and starts discussing them, he finds a resolution. Now, this is also the process of psychoanalysis, but here it is not about the mind alone: it's about the larger existence, which involves the higher consciousness of the universe itself. It is very egoistic for man to think that he's the only creature in this whole wondrous creation with consciousness. It simply cannot be that man is the only thing with a sensitive conscious. In order to create man's consciousness itself, it is incumbent that there must be some higher energy, some higher power. And spirituality is to be in a flow with that higher power. But in order to be in a flow with that higher power, it is required of us to be completely aware—with all our energies—of that which is restricting us in life and to try and go into it. Going into it itself will dilute the problems in your life.

Let's take an example: that which made us fearful as children were the dark corners, the unknown. Darkness meant fear, light meant release from that fear! So similarly, the moment you şhine the light of consciousness upon the unknown, it stops being fearful to you! In the same way, Arjun comes out refreshed, courageous, with a much richer sense of soul than when he began his questions.

It is all about a question of inner expansion. If you want to expand in any way—for example, you want to expand the effectiveness of your work life, or expand the scope of your relationships, or expand your understanding of things spiritual or cosmic—always begin with asking! Do not hesitate to confront those things which are problematic in your life. Else they remain somewhere deep in your consciousness and keep troubling you. They do not allow you to grow. You see, every plant begins just as a seed under the soil, but in order for it to evolve it has to burst out of the soil! To face the sunlight. And that sunlight itself will dynamize and energize it. But if in the beginning it had been exposed to sunlight, it would have died. Yet when it finds enough strength plus courage to break out of the soil, is when the sunlight starts having a positive effect on it.

Arjun has within himself been in a state of turmoil, a state where he's not sure of what will happen. But as he breaks out of his shell and moves towards the sunlight of higher consciousness through the Lord's answers, he becomes energized. And becoming energized, he finds the strength to confront whatever he's faced with, most fearlessly! It is a question eventually of courage. Without that quality we cannot move towards an understanding of the eternal. And neither can we move towards a state of fearless living.

One of the most blessed things in life is to function from a state of fearlessness. If you can do that in whatever you do, you will find yourself becoming infinitely more effective and more powerful in your actions. You will not fall back again and again because of fears. Therefore, it becomes increasingly important for us to understand that the whole journey begins with spiritual questions! Never hesitate to ask them, never hesitate to probe into them. It is the perfect way to establish a relationship with the higher dimension of the divine, because you are sharing that which is in your heart. And when you do that, you'll find such effective answers, and be filled with such bliss and strength, that you yourself will be surprised!

CHAPTER-18

The Gita Enables Clarity of Consciousness

The whole art of brilliance in action lies in the ability to see things clearly, without disturbances and distractions: to directly see in a manner which gives you a very lucid understanding. And for that, one thing is needed: we are to give up those thoughts which distort our view of the world. We are to renounce unnecessary thoughts. Most of our thoughts are useless: they only stop us from seeing with full clarity of the consciousness. Thoughts can disturb the consciousness, and in disturbance of the consciousness arises not only a poor understanding of things but also a poor understanding of life itself, plus of our own being. The very basis of lack of quality in life is this unclear understanding of life and of one's being's vaster spiritual dimensions. Being *clear* in consciousness is the fundamental step towards dealing with tough times.

People often think it is a 'belief system' which shapes our lives; but it's the clarity of consciousness, or the lack of it, which shapes our lives. That requires renouncing unnecessary thoughts, which is a very important aspect of the Gita. This is what Krishna is constantly telling Arjun: that he's not to be entangled with the concerns of the mind. He is to surrender the assertions of the mind. Then only will he come to a state which is ecstatic and blissful. Only when he lays down his thoughts and surrenders them to Krishna—to life itself—is when he'll have the courage to pick up the bow and fight as an ace archer on the battlefield. Hence, this is immensely important for us to understand: that it's all coming back to a state of consciousness which is non-corrupted by stray thoughts. Therein lies greater understanding, greater calmness, greater glimpses of the temple of life or the shrine of God within.

The prayerful state and the devoted state is the courageous state. But this state cannot be achieved by non-renunciation of thoughts. It comes only where there is innocence, it comes only where there is clarity. Spirituality is not morality: it is instead all about seeing things *as they are*, and to step out of our insanity of the material world. And doing that, we attain a great inner silence. We attain a situation where we are not distracted. Where we are receptive to greater energies, sensitive to them, and enhanced in our power to function within the world.

So, renunciation of thought has a great penetrating power. Nothing else can substitute it. It allows us to melt and flow into the cosmic consciousness: that is the ultimate experience. It allows us to rejoice in life.

The Gita is constantly a reminder that all our habits of overthinking can be made to disappear if only we have this one attitude: of surrendering and renouncing thoughts. Of letting go of them. And seeing what lies in the most subtle domain—beyond our ordinary thoughts. Most of our thoughts are of the gross elements in life. They bring us into a conflict with existence. They bring us to a state of contrariness, where we are constantly in aggression, where we are constantly in a situation where joy is prevented from arising within us. To attain the greater genuineness of self requires renunciation of thoughts. In a person to whom that happens, the very body language changes, the very charisma and presence of the person changes. Because then the person becomes a channel for the greater energy which is flowing throughout the cosmos. You can call that energy the Divine, you can call that energy the power of the Source. Ultimately, it is simply a situation where the person is aligned to the greater consciousness—what we might call the Krishna-consciousness, or God-consciousness. That is the state where your consciousness is aligned to the divine consciousness, and is not surrounded or held captive only by what you are thinking. What you are thinking is very small compared to the fullness of things: it is not a necessary part of evolution and growth. Instead, you are to enter the stream of the meditative state. And that stream is one of wakefulness, that stream is one where all your dreams have been shattered against the rock of the Divine. And instead of thoughts you are filled with bliss, clarity, energy, vitality, and a natural power which has come out of the mutual respect between you and life. You then become a more essential and valuable part of life, and life goes on filling you with all that is vital and essential.

The only difference between a person of clarity and a person of confusion is this ability: the ability to renounce thoughts. The only difference between a person who is a procrastinator (one who constantly postpones things) and a person of intensity (one who takes action in the present instant) is this ability: to renounce thoughts. Arjun has become a procrastinator, and Krishna is bringing him back to intensity in action. Where there is intensity, useless thoughts completely evaporate. Just like water evaporates under the light of the Sun! The light of the Gita has the power to make you more natural in your functioning, to open your heart into a situation where you perceive from it. Man has become very closed—his heart is not very open. His mind is full. And the heart has almost shrunk in its functioning. By 'heart' is meant the centre of being, the greater consciousness. And once a person gets his heart involved in something, naturally, passion comes about and energy comes about. Clarity comes about. One quality of the heart is that it transcends ordinary thought. Hence, it is always about opening up your heart and being from within. It is always about unification between yourself and the greater universe. This is very essential for us to understand as far as the Gita goes. What it is teaching you is not about moral 'character'; what it is teaching you is about destroying that which is non-essential! And that which is non-essential is simply *conditioned thought*! It is the past, it is the manner of thinking with the ego, the manner of utilizing the mind to look into all aspects of reality. But because reality is too vast, all aspects of it cannot be understood through thoughts. Make your heart less hard; make it more sensitive. And allow yourself to perceive from its deepest depths. Then only can you attain that level of devotion which Krishna is talking about, that level of courage and fullness in action which he is trying to awaken Arjun into. Then do you come into harmony within yourself and with the greater reality. Else, you are completely isolated as an individual.

Arjun has become an island—he is not able to function with the wholeness of harmony that is required of him. He has become contracted within his own mind. And Krishna opens him up, and the wisdom floods Arjun's heart and mind. They open up. He is taken away from the paralysis of his own thoughts and into the pure light of consciousness, which is his birthright! And which indeed is the birthright of every conscious being. It is the peak of ourselves. It is the universe speaking to us. It is the universe calling out to us to understand our own pulse, to understand our own basic state of enlightenment which always lies beyond the realm of ordinary thoughts.

One has to cast away thoughts: thoughts are repetitive, so if we keep living in the same thoughts and giving them new life, we reach nowhere. Because we do not move towards the new, we do not move towards the fresh, we do not move towards the most intrinsic parts of our being. We only use thoughts as an ego exercise, to justify ourselves—our position, power, wealth and so on. Krishna's whole attitude is the complete opposite: he takes us to the closest part of our true beings, and to the closest part of the cosmic reality.

Basically, instead of relying on an egoistic understanding of the universe, it's time for us to become part of that flow which is full of wonder. Full of the mystic element. And therefore, full of the joy of living in a much deeper way! Thoughts themselves cannot generate joy in the way that our sense of wonder and our inner dance with bliss in this beautiful universe can do. Thoughts are a very poor substitute for completeness of participation as cosmic citizens in this wondrous universe! And intelligence is not about being able to repeat that which has been taught to us. But rather it is always about moving towards the new, and pulsating with the harmony of the vast. That is also true religion: the ability to transform all that we know into something higher.

Knowledge becomes self-defeating if it is not transmuted into higher knowing. It becomes a poison in us because it gets transformed into ego. And this is what Krishna is warning Arjun against: he does not want Arjun to get into the trifles of ego. He wants him to only know that knowledge which is of real worth. And that knowledge, which is of real worth, is the knowledge of devotion. It is of renouncing thoughts. It is of surrendering to the greater state of being. It is the ability to have a vision which is full of wonder and awe for the tremendousness of life that we are part of, and to find real meaning and real positive feeling in that. Most of the time, thoughts create negativity in us:

if you examine your own thoughts you'd see that they create a cycle of negativity more often than they create a cycle of positiveness. Hence, what is the hesitation in dropping them? They do not serve us either at an individual level, at a mystic level, or spiritual level. And ultimately don't even help our relationships or our work. When it comes to work people think it's all about thought-skills. Actually it's about being able to drop the negative parts of yourself and allowing your natural ability to flow as positively as possible. And that also requires us to function freely, without the burden of over-excessive thought. You'd notice that some of the most dynamic leaders are not overly analytical. But they have a great energy, which has the ability to influence others. So if you wish to be a positive influence upon others, do remember this principle of the importance of clarity over over-analysis.

The whole of life can have a different quality if you have this vision, and if you can see that in the renunciation of thoughts you can walk stronger, stand taller, get rid of all the complexes which have plagued you! Then you would see that your energies become crystallized at your very core, and your focus becomes strong and single-minded! You're able to achieve things much faster and quicker, because your brain is not split into the thousands of thoughts which may be distracting you.

Clarity in action is always a question of renouncing extra thoughts that can cloud the power of the action. The very basis of focus lies in eliminating that which is not required. And eliminating that which is not required is essentially a lesson about doing away with those mental impulses which sap us of energy. Utilize the mind, but don't be utilized by it: this is what Krishna is telling Arjun. He tells him very clearly that the mind is like the wind: a very powerful force! It takes man onto whatever direction it wants. But the problem is that we don't have enough spiritual wherewithal to be the masters of mind: if you are the master, well and good. Otherwise it's better to drop the mind and its myriad mental activities which may be having an effect on you, and instead assume the attitude of surrender. In this attitude of surrender, what automatically happens is that you feel filled with the divinity of energy. And all that is negative in you starts emptying. Very often the mind can be a heap of rubbish: it keeps collecting things. It becomes a big garbage can, and to clear this garbage can is to realize the fragrance of life in a far stronger manner. It is to realize that you can proceed with great energy in whatever direction you want, when you are lighter in your being, when you are lighter in the mind.

The whole art of opening doors of life (so that you move on to new paths) lies in the act of being prayerful. And real prayerfulness can never be found within a person who is full of contradictory thoughts. You see, the thing about thoughts is that they breed contradictions. They emotionally disturb us. They make us believe in all sorts of ideas which may not necessarily be true. Hence, most of them are not of any worth at all. They rather may take us away from our inner truth, and make us neurotic. The thing about the mind is that it has a process of creating all sorts of emotions which might not be suitable for us: for example, the feeling of anger, the feeling of guilt, and so on. And you'd find that the more subtle feelings—like those of love—are almost beyond thought! We are surprised when they happen! They come as a gift of life itself. And that is a very natural process.

In the world of the mystical, all that is truly good comes as a gift. All that is really great comes as a part of worship. That is the meaningfulness of life. The other side is anxiety, anguish, and to become a person who keeps running after things but essentially misses that which is already within oneself! Thoughts make us go from one impulse to the other; they make us run after things and hanker after things. But the whole spiritual attitude—the attitude of both the sage and the enlightened warrior—is of internalization. To such an extent that all strength is absorbed into one's own being, into one's own mentation, into one's own heart. And from there, whatever action comes becomes extremely dynamic. That is what is happening in the Gita: Arjun's action is becoming more and more dynamic, as he's able to cut out the process of anxious thought from his mind. It is like cutting out the roots of suffering, literally.

You can look at all spiritual paths—they encode this kind of truth very often. You can look at the Buddhist path: Gautama Buddha taught his disciples to watch their thoughts, and through watching the thoughts itself, most of them drop off on their own, thereby leading to a greater synthesis in being. Most evil acts on earth have been committed because of having wrong thoughts. Yes, there have been great mental achievements of man, but those have not necessarily come out of limited thoughts; they have come out of 'eureka' moments or instants of inspiration. Almost as if life itself has spoken to the inventor or to the discoverer, who has been struggling hard. And through such inspiration have been found great sources of light, great breakthroughs for the good of society, and so on.

So, inspirational thought is in a slightly different dimension, because it also has an element of the mystical. Inspirational thought is always useful, because it has a connection with the deeper portions of life itself. But ordinary thought—which is often simply the processing of our latent anxieties and preconditioned notions about things—takes away the essence of spiritual purity which is within us. At the heart of us lies great brilliance: to touch that brilliance requires us to scrape off the dust which is covering it. That dust is often in the shape of thoughts, in the shape of ideas and stories which we have imposed upon ourselves. You see, the mind is a great maker of stories. But through making stories, it can often take you off your true path. The heart is a true judge of the path that you might be walking upon. The heart is your inner voice: you can call it your voice of conscience.

But it is not so much about 'brain versus heart'. That is a very puerile and childlike discussion. When we talk about consciousness it is not about the organ of consciousness; it is about the quality of consciousness. Of whether your ideation has come out of ordinary mental conditioning, or it has come out of a greater root within the universe, within life itself, within the greater wisdom of things.

Spontaneous thoughts and spontaneous emotions—those which embrace the concepts of harmony, compassion, friendliness and so on—are positive. They'll always help. But the problem is that man very often is a contradiction within himself: because with light comes darkness, with positive thoughts come negative thoughts. The whole science of Vedanta and the science of the Gita itself is a very definitive spiritual science, because it tells us to cut the root of thought itself. So that positive and negative don't remain. Then, whatever happens, happens as a will of the Divine.

The Gita talks about the essence of things. It doesn't mean that a person is to stop thinking: rather, the teaching can be likened to removing the blocks from the flow of water. Meaning this: let's say you want water to flow nicely and there's something blocking it, like an obstruction or a dam. If you remove that block, the water will flow again. So that is the way our energy has been defined in Vedanta: the flow of water. And sometimes the only 'blocks' we put on that energy are these blocks of thoughts. Thoughts can block our energy in a manner which does not allow us to inwardly unite with and be in harmony with the greater truth of life. Thoughts often do not allow us to come into a greater contact with universal wisdom which is all around us: we can call it nature, God, Divine, we can also call it the universal parents. In whatever shape or form we wish, it is all about emphasizing the fullness of life. If we're connected to the fullness of life, we become wise, deep, and more unconditional in our actions. So doing, we find ourselves more ready for whatever challenges life throws up!

The most fearful people are sometimes those who overthink things. You would have seen it in your own friends: there are some people who are constantly fearful about things. About what will happen tomorrow: they might get a disease, somebody might die, the economy might get spoiled, and so on. These are people who constantly look at problems which *might* arise. While it's good to be cautious, what happens is that such a thought process develops into a phobia of the mind. It becomes a great block in the flow of energy. Such people will always sap your energy. On the other hand there are some people who are spontaneous in action: you'd find their energy much more positive. They create a vibe of joy and they uplift you when you are with them!

Basically, you need to be ready to transform yourself through the ability of renouncing thoughts. All of us have responsibilities in life, but the burden of responsibility does not become necessarily better by taking on the burden of more and more thoughts. Sometimes it is good to release our energy: to go into a great emptiness. This is what the Hindus have called the state of *shunyata*, where you're simply in flow with life itself. And being in that blissful flow, you find that it becomes easier to cross the stream, it becomes easier to climb the mountain, it becomes easier to feel the energy of the Divine. And to experience the delight of passion which takes you onward and upward in your personal quest in life, whatever it may be. Past all barriers of circumstances!

CHAPTER-19

Death

In what is now a very famous speech, Steve Jobs of Apple Inc. addressed students of Stanford University and told them that he finds the question of death to be the most awakening factor in life. In a nutshell, what he was saying was really an echo of the Gita. Jobs said that if you confront the question of death all that is really important comes into sharp focus. And then you do all that which is really important, fearlessly! The understanding and realization of death is key to living past tough times with higher consciousness and dynamic action.

Remember, the great person always moves towards a higher consciousness when the prospect of death becomes real! Most people move into a state of fear, into a state of inwardness when death comes. The fact of death is fearful. Yes, that's natural. But eventually, the highest teachings can only be disseminated through the fact of death. You can look at the Indian scripture called the Katha Upanishad: it is a very important text in Hindu thought, in Sanatan Dharma. It's the conversation between Nachiketa the boy and Yamraj (Yama) himself: Death personified, the lord of death, Dharmaraj! Ultimately, the entire philosophy of the Vedas, the Upanishads, the Vedanta, the *Sankhya,* has all been distilled into the Katha Upanishad. It's all about how to face death. It is all about life *and* death. Death, personified as Yama, is the greatest teacher (as can be seen in this enlightening sacred text, the Katha Upanishad). This is meant to teach us that even in the face of the biggest challenge, that of dying, we can move towards wisdom, bliss, spiritual enlightenment!

Now, Krishna is telling Arjun that death is not something which he has to grieve over: whether his own death or whether his enemies' deaths, or whether that of his friends'.

So, the first step towards freedom is this acceptance: where you can see that life and death are simply two sides of the same coin. Then you are able to become a risk-taker. Only then can you stake everything for that which is really important. Otherwise we are just drifting through life, not really serious. But eventually it's not even a question of seriousness; it's a question of how much the element of play itself can come into life. How effortlessly we can achieve things. How we can be blissful within. It all comes back to this fear of death. All other fears in life are related to this fear. If you examine yourself deeply you'd find that eventually it is the greatest fear: whether it's dying of disease, dying of calamity, or contemplating our dear ones' deaths. This is always the crux upon which our life revolves. And the fear of it makes us commit all of the wrongs that we commit in life.

A person who is truly strong before the question of death and is in total acceptance of it can never really go wrong, because all he does becomes vitally correct. All he does is in tandem with the great universal flow of things. It is very interesting that Gautama Buddha says that we come from nothingness and go to nothingness. Everything is a great void, and human life is just a play of cosmic phenomena which makes us mentally come under the illusion that there is something to be done and something not to be done. In the end, as the Gita says, all is being done already! The galaxies are revolving, the universe is moving. Yet the human being thinks that all is being done because of himself. And that he's a doer of things. This very idea is wrong. Be dead to this idea and then you truly awaken to that which is life-fulfilling!

In a way the whole Gita is a discourse on death. Krishna is making those elements of Arjun die which make him fearful, which make him shirk from responsibilities. He is awakening those qualities which truly bring the timeless qualities of Arjun alive.

Eventually, the highest spiritual scriptures always deal with death. But you have to remember to go away from childish notions about reward and punishment, 'Judgment Day' and all that nonsense. Move from all that takes you away from the essential evolution of consciousness. Remember, teachings which are rooted in mere belief systems will never reach to those great heights which *teachings about consciousness* reach up to. Consciousness-teachings are the way of Sanatan Dharma, consciousness-teachings are the way of Tantra, consciousness-teachings are the way of Zen Buddhism. So, therein you would find mature spirituality.

Also, you will find this in the spirituality of Kabir, the spirituality of Guru Nanak, the spirituality of Zoroaster, the spirituality of Baba Gorakhnath. These fundamentally deal with the question of death as much as they do about *living* spiritually.

The more you die to the unnecessary, the more you awaken to the necessary. This is the golden rule when it comes to things of spirituality. Usually, we are more awake to those things which are not important and dead to those things which are less important. How many people have the burning question within them of who they are, where they come from, and such vital questions of life! Most of us are just moving from one day of the calendar to the next without really delving into the roots of life itself. And at the roots of life lies the question of birth, but even more importantly lies the question of death: because that is the space from which the endless begins. Contemplating death is really the ultimate spiritual exercise you can undertake.

You can take any sage or seer in the world,

and you would find that at their very heart is the transcendence of the fear of death. Else, fear keeps lingering around us, as a constant. We are so often physically scared, intellectually scared, spiritually scared. To be liberated from fear in all directions is really the whole question that the Gita seeks answers to. And so doing seeks to bring clarity into the mind.

The deeper into death you go, the deeper your experience of life is. The less into death you go, the more shallow your life is. It is an inverse relationship. So, in order to listen to the innermost voice within us (and to the innermost voice in all of creation), to live with genuineness, we have to go into the question of death. This is really at the heart and the crux of life. It is really about going beyond happiness, it is really about being able to find that passion and intensity of living which is beyond the destructive power on the physical plane.

Krishna is telling Arjun again and again that nothing can destroy that which is timeless. So, through that lesson you come to the belief that you can be truly blissful in life, that you can be truly filled with an aliveness of spirit, and that there is nothing which can be taken away from you!

The main problem which people have is that of insecurity. The more richly endowed a person is at a material level, the more fearful they often become. A person who doesn't have much is not very fearful: how much can he lose! Only the little he has. And he can start again. But the person who has much, has much to lose also. In that manner Arjun is at a crossroads, because he has a reputation, he has riches, he has a following, he has people who respect him. And all that can be lost! Most importantly, he stands to lose the enormous gift of friends and family which he is endowed with. So he comes to a moment of insecurity. And Krishna takes him away from that insecurity, and towards a feeling that, essentially, nothing is secure in life. 'We are already moving towards death', so where is the question of insecurity or security.

Krishna takes away this false illusion that we are completely secure. But he also reassures Arjun that in the mystic sense we are always secure, because we really cannot be destroyed. So it's a pro-life discourse, but ironically, it is said in a language which makes it seem anti-life. That is the mystic beauty of the Gita: it might say one thing in words, but it means something much deeper. It leads to a great spontaneity of joy, it makes us drown in the waters of the mystical. And only in drowning in those waters is the true resurrection possible. This is almost reminiscent of the resurrection of Jesus of Nazareth in the Middle East: only through death does resurrection come, does faith in the higher come. Without it there will be no real faith in the higher power. Similarly, Krishna says it is essential to confront the question of death because without it there can be no realization of what life really means. And if you have accepted death, everything else looks playful, everything else looks like less of a challenge. Everything else can be confronted with great courage. The most courageous people are those who can transcend the fear of death, because then they become spontaneously dynamic; they become spontaneously and effortlessly courageous. Nothing can deter you or make you fearful once you have transcended the most essential question, and that is of course the question of being able to lose all things in an instant: all attachments, all riches, this very body itself.

That is the true spirit of the warrior and that is the only way that human evolution and growth can happen. Psychologically, it is the most challenging barrier, but if you can overcome this challenge then only do the doors and windows of your consciousness open to the feeling that you can live spontaneously, that you can go beyond all pretensions. And going beyond all pretensions is the way to transcend all self-conflict and to have the guts to meet conflicts in everyday life.

It is all a question of the responsibility a person can bear; a person who cannot even confront the question of death but is constantly escaping from it has no way to make life less of a burden. For such a person everything in life becomes a burden, because there is a lingering fear. Only a person who is liberated of that fear ceases to look at life as a burden, and finds that there is no need to be miserable. Eventually, everything is already lost! The only joy we can find is in what is here and now, and in what power we have through functioning in this present instant.

Man is a creature of fantasies. He keeps imagining things. Arjun keeps imagining that what is going to happen is against all conscience, against all morality. Arjun, like us, is a creature of conditioning. He is very puritan in his view: he is condemning that which he feels is evil, violence.

But he doesn't realize that if he does not confront this evil violence through the act of confronting death, then there can be no transcendence of this evil violence. Sometimes, to buy peace, violence is needed. And that is why it becomes necessary that this battle is rightly fought. Then only will Arjun's actions through his life have any value. Otherwise his whole life as a warrior would have been a waste, because he would have failed when he was really wanted. So, Krishna is bringing Arjun to a real unity with his own self. And also to an understanding of what it means to look behind the curtain of life.

Death is a mystery: it seems the truth of it is 'behind the curtain'. Arjun is simply opening the curtain through Krishna's words, and then he finds that there was no need for him to be so perplexed. Then he finds that it is an astonishingly rejuvenating and relaxing feeling to be able to destroy the unnecessary fear of death coming to one's loved ones and to oneself. Once that garbage is cleared, once that uncensored process is cleared, Arjun feels an unburdening of all his anxieties. And through this feeling of unburdening he is able to move towards an expression of his own power, strength, and innate beauty. Through the art of battle.

Everybody has a different way of expressing their innate potentiality and the innate beauty of their skill. Arjun's skill lies in the art of the warrior. In a way, everybody is a warrior, because everybody has the power to bring the light of consciousness onto the darkness of the question of death. And when you shine that light of consciousness upon the darkness of death, then you find that its fear starts going away. The darkness is gone, the fear is gone, and you feel a great alchemy within your being.

What is alchemy? Alchemy is taking one thing and transforming it into something much more valuable. So here, alchemy is really the question of death. If you can transform your understanding of this one thing called death, it becomes pure gold. It helps you on your search for a more purposeful life. It brings grace in your life. It brings harmony, power, and strength in your life. Then you move on in a manner you had never done before in your life: you proceed with joy, a ring in your step. You proceed with a feeling that all things are possible. You proceed in a manner where you feel that the greatest experiences can happen to you, also because you are now in harmony with the truly deep spiritual question of life.

The problem with organized religion is that while it talks about so many things, when it talks about death, it's usually very childish. Because it talks about the afterlife in a manner where you are rewarded or punished for what you have done on earth. Whereas it should be a question of unconditioning you from the fear of death. If it manages to do that then you come into a spiritual unification with your own being. That is the true and essential thing about death. And then you find that you can go beyond the chaos and find an inner harmony, inner grace, and an inner Moksha/Nirvana or feeling of free enlightenment.

In the old tradition of Indian religions there used to be a system of sending novices or new monks to the cremation grounds to observe bodies being cremated. To watch the physical being flowing into the basic elements. The observance of death was part of the essential mind training and spiritual training of all religions. Because that itself creates a bit of a synthesis, and takes away the fundamental feeling of boundary between life and death. You start understanding that the physical body only changes form, but there is something else which can happen on the search which is beyond this physical body. And that is what ecstasy is. That is what the timeless instant of spiritual realization is, that is when great inner silence can come about. Ultimately, this facing of the question leads you to a meditative, joyful, and blissful state such as you have never known.

Eventually, through the Gita, Krishna is taking Arjun onto a path where he can become that great dynamic movement of energy which he has always been as a warrior. The whole movement of energy has stopped in Arjun because of his anxiety over death. But now through the Gita his potentiality starts growing naturally, starts going higher, starts becoming playful and forceful. You can imagine him feeling empowered after the Gita and adopting a more holistic attitude not only towards life, not only towards the divine, but towards the question of destruction and the question of death itself. Krishna describes himself as the 'destroyer of worlds', and Arjun comes to see that without destruction, the cycle of creation itself cannot move forward. It is like the statue of Shiva—the dancing Shiva or Nataraj—which portrays a whole cycle of creation and destruction. Everything is cyclical in nature. For the new to happen the old must go, and so on. Through this understanding Arjun's mind is lit up with the feeling that everything is okay; there is nothing he needs to be so perplexed about. This whole overemphasis on anxiety will drive Arjun insane: he comes to see that and he realizes that there is no point banging the head against a fact which is going to happen anyway. Which is death. So, accepting it is really the way out, and then you are ready to encounter anything in life. And if you are ready to encounter anything in life, you spontaneously move towards success. It is a real breakthrough.

So, the whole transformation is from Arjun's question of mental breakdown into the question of moving forward in a manner where he attains clear understanding, clear alertness, and a clear ability to do that which needs to be done. But with a feeling of devotion, not with a feeling of ill-will or violence. Functioning in that manner, Arjun has come to a realization of the divine which is existent within us.

The enlightened soul is one who has attained a profound silence, where even the question of death does not disturb the silence. That is the whole test of enlightened living. You can feel the timeless perspective of yourself, as that perspective resides within us as our inner being. This is the true transformation of spirituality, where even death transforms into a passionate quest for that which is higher, that which is more important, and that which cannot be taken away. So, all awakening in life is really a question of not having just the right philosophy or worldview of life, but of struggling and breaking free of the grip of death on our being. And the grip of death is really a psychological one. It is one of fear. It is one of making us smaller than we are. It is one which prevents us from experiencing the silent vastness and stillness of our own consciousness. In the end, it's all about being able to listen to our own vastness of consciousness, and in order to do that it becomes imperative that we do not give in to the fear of death. That we accept it as it is and see that all of creation is a dream where we come and go, but the uniqueness of existence itself remains. This dream-like quality of all existence is poignantly described in Hindu mysticism: from Lord Garbhodakshayi Vishnu, resting on the waters of the eternal ocean of ultimate reality and dreaming the cosmic dream, arise billions of Brahmas or universal creators, one following the other.

We are mere players in this unique creation, and need to feel privileged that we have been given an opportunity to participate in it in the manner that we have been. So doing, you'll find that nothing will disturb you. So doing, you'll find that you become a pure witness (in a joyful and blissful state) to all the beauty and all the opportunity that is surrounding you. If you can contemplate this even for a few moments, you would find that all your distorted anxieties can disappear, and you become more capable of seeing things as they are in their purity! And not only that, you become capable of radiating the light of your own potential in a much greater manner. Because you have been able to disassociate yourself from the fear of death itself!

Never give the question of death so much power over you that it brings you to your knees psychologically or emotionally. It has literally brought Arjun to his knees, and the whole of the Gita is Krishna picking up Arjun from his knees, of washing him clean of all fears and allowing his consciousness to ascend spiritually to the highest Himalayan heights. And from there, Arjun sees a totally different view of man! He sees a totally different view of life, and becomes dynamized not only from within, but as a warrior. As a person who can fulfil his tasks in life fearlessly. True heroism in life means the ability to awaken to the challenge of death.

All through history, it is those martyrs, it is those people who have faced the gallows or faced death with courage who are the highest kind of human beings. You can look at Socrates of Greece, you can look at Jesus Christ or the Sikh gurus, and so many others over the ages! And you would find this one essential quality in all such beings: that the urge to associate life with the length of years has evaporated in them. They are content to have lived as much as they have, because they know that beyond the physical activity of the body lies that realm which is timeless and deathless, both. And in that realm dwell the Buddhas. In that realm dwells the power of Krishna. In that realm dwells the eternal bliss of the Absolute. So become a part of it, become more identified with that vastness beyond the physical bounds of the body. Then you would find that there is something indestructible in you, then you would find that there's something immensely valuable in you. Realizing this immense value in you, you begin to feel a capacity which perhaps you've never ever felt before. Feeling this, you're able to explore your talent. You're able to explore your potential in a much deeper manner than you would have ever thought possible. Nothing can disturb you, nothing can take away the eternal feeling of peace within you, once you have been able to connect your consciousness with that eternal principle which is the foundation and bedrock of all things.

Man's mind moves between extremes: sometimes it becomes extremely fearful, and sometimes it becomes extremely proud, as if nothing can happen to him. Krishna is in a way stripping off both extremes of Arjun: he's taking away his pride, bringing him to his knees (surrendering). Showing him that he, Krishna, determines all things, and not human beings. In other words, the divine element determines things. But on the other hand, Krishna is stripping away Arjun of his mindless fear of death. Our fear of death itself—whether it's of ourselves or our loved ones—needs to go because that is the one stumbling block which makes even the most powerful warrior become absolutely weak and useless. So through this dual exercise (surrender and fearlessness) is the doorway to the divine; to the achievement of higher potentiality within us and to human excellence. No matter how tough things get, we can proceed towards fulfilling our infinite potential through such spiritual understanding and enlightenment!

Acknowledgements

I wish to express my humble gratitude to the people who have made this series possible:

Anuj Bahri, my super literary agent at Red Ink.

Shikha Sabharwal and Gaurav Sabharwal, my wonderful publishers at Fingerprint! Publishing and their team.

Garima Shukla, my amazing and brilliant editor.

Family: my parents Anita and Jeet Gupta, partner Sohini, sister Priti, brother-in-law Manish, niece Vaanee, nephew Kartikay, cousins, aunts, and uncles. You are my rock!

Gratitude also to my many Gurus and mentors, school batchmates and teachers (St Paul's School, Darjeeling), and friends.

Pranay is a mystic philosopher. He is an expert on Indian and world spirituality.

Pranay's modules on 'Advanced Spirituality for Leadership and Success' (PowerTalks/MysticTalks for public and corporate audiences) have won global acclaim.

Pranay is also a theatre personality and playwright. His original productions such as *From Kabir to Kavi* and *Soul Stir* have been acclaimed by world luminaries for their path-breaking spiritual content.

Pranay and his partner Sohini run the socio-cultural philanthropic commune TAS, whose initiatives such as 'Theatre Against Drugs' (for addicts), 'Geetimalya' (for underprivileged children) and 'Shohaag' (for women empowerment) are well-known and have become movements.

Presently, Pranay is collating his discourses on mind-body-spirit themes for various book series.

Connect with him on his website: pranay.org